SEARCHING FOR THE TRUTH

QUOTATIONS FROM THE WISDOM OF THE AGES

Compiled by Margaret Herrick

Illustrations by Katherine Drucklieb

Exposition Press New York

EXPOSITION PRESS INC.

386 Park Avenue South New York, N.Y. 10016

FIRST EDITION

 Manufactured in the United States of America. Library of Congress catalogue-card number: 67-29056.

EP 46784

To

Katherine Drucklieb

and

Lorraine Ridge

ACKNOWLEDGMENTS

FOR arrangements made with various publishing houses whereby permission to reprint excerpts from copyrighted material has been granted, and for the courtesy extended by them and by several authors and others, the following acknowledgments are gratefully made:

Constable and Company Limited, London, for quotations from *William Blake, His Philosophy and Symbols,* by S. Damon Foster (Boston: Houghton Mifflin Company, 1924).

Miss D. E. Collins and Doubleday & Co., Inc., for quotations from *St. Francis of Assisi,* by G. K. Chesterton. Copyright 1925 by Gilbert Keith Chesterton; renewed 1953.

The Curtis Publishing Company, for quotations from "I Always Have Help," which appeared in *The Saturday Evening Post,* May 21, 1960. Copyright 1960 The Curtis Publishing Company.

The Dial Press, for the quotation reprinted from *That Day Alone,* by Pierre Van Paassen. Copyright 1941 by Pierre Van Paassen and used with the permission of the publisher, The Dial Press, Inc.

Joseph Dunninger, for quotations from his *What's on Your Mind?* (New York: World Publishing Company, 1944).

Harcourt, Brace & World, Inc., for quotations from *Europe,* by Count Hermann Keyserling, translated by Maurice Samuel, copyright, 1928, by Harcourt, Brace and World, Inc.; renewed, 1956, by Maurice Samuel. Reprinted by permission of the publisher. —And for quotations from *The Travel Diary of a Philosopher,* by Count Hermann Keyserling, translated by J. Holroyd Reece, copyright, 1925, by Harcourt, Brace and World, Inc.; renewed, 1953, by J. Holroyd Reece. Reprinted by permission of the publisher.

Harper & Row, Publishers, for quotations from *On Being a Real Person,* by Harry Emerson Fosdick (Harper & Brothers, 1943). Reprinted by permission of Harper & Row, Publishers. —And for quotations from four books by Count Hermann Keyserling: *America Set Free; Creative Understanding; Recovery of the Truth;* and *The World in the Making.* Reprinted by permission of Harper & Row, Publishers.

David Higham Associates, Ltd., London, for quotations from Francis Yeats-Brown, *Lancer at Large* (London: Dennis Dobson, 1938).

Holt, Rinehart and Winston, Inc., for quotations from *Out of My Life and Thought,* by Albert Schweitzer. Translated by C. T. Campion. Copyright, 1933, 1949, by Holt, Rinehart and Winston, Inc. Reprinted here by permission of Holt, Rinehart and Winston, Inc.

Houghton Mifflin Company, for the quotation from *The Dance of Life,* by Havelock Ellis (1923). —And for quotations from *Sibelius,* by Bengt de Torne (1937).

Countess Goedela Keyserling, for quotations from *Problems of Personal Life* and other books by Count Hermann Keyserling, and for excerpts from notes taken by the compiler at various lectures by Count Keyserling. (Note: Quotations from lecture notes may not be verbatim excerpts; they may have been somewhat paraphrased in transmission.)

David McKay Company, Inc., for quotations from *Human Destiny,* by Lecomte du Noüy, © copyright, 1947. Used by permission of David McKay Company, Inc.

The Macmillan Company, New York, for quotations from *Sadhana,* by Rabindranath Tagore. Copright, 1913, by the Macmillan Company; renewed, 1941, by Rabindranath Tagore.

The New York Times and R. L. Duffus, for the quotation from his review that appeared in *The New York Times Book Review* on December 12, 1937.

The New York Times and A. D. Peters & Company, London, for the quotation from "Rain Upon Godshill," by J. B. Priestley, which appeared in *The New York Times Book Review* on October 29, 1939.

W. W. Norton & Company, Inc., for the quotation from

R.F.D., by Charles Allen Smart, copyright, 1938; renewed, 1965.

A. D. Peters & Company, London, for the quotation from "The Minor Pleasures of Life," by J. B. Priestley, which appeared in *The Reader's Digest* on October 1, 1939.

Putnam's & Coward-McCann, for quotations from *Goethe: The History of a Man,* by Emil Ludwig, translated from the German by Ethel Colburn Mayne (1928).

Putnam's & Coward-McCann, and Mrs. Lewis E. Lawes, for quotations from *Life and Death in Sing Sing,* by Lewis E. Lawes (1924).

Random House, Inc., for the quotation from the English version of *Dr. Zhivago,* by Boris Pasternak.

Random House, Inc./Alfred A. Knopf, Inc., for the quotation from *The Magic Mountain,* by Thomas Mann, translated by H. T. Lowe-Porter. Copyright 1927 and renewed 1955 by Alfred A. Knopf, Inc. Reprinted by permission. —And for quotations from *The Romance of Leonardo da Vinci,* by Dmitri Merejkowski, translated by Bernard Guilbert Guerney. Copyright 1928 and renewed 1955 by Modern Library, Inc. Reprinted by permission of Random House, Inc. —And for the excerpts from *Tertium Organum,* by P. D. Ouspensky, translated by N. Bessaraboff and Claude Bragdon. Copyright 1920 by Manas Press; copyright 1922 by Claude Bragdon. Reprinted by permission of Alfred A. Knopf, Inc.

The Reader's Digest, for quotations from "Heredity: The Hope of Mankind," by Bruce Blivens, published in May, 1941; "The Most Unforgettable Character I've Met," by Manuel Komroff, April, 1941; "A Sand County Almanac," by Aldo Leopold, March, 1961; and a quotation from George Washington Carver.

Saturday Night, for the quotation from "Tsk, Tsk—Sudbury Is Only Froth," by H. Dyoon Carter, which appeared on March 14, 1941. Reprinted by permission of the editor.

Science Service Inc., for quotations from *The Advance of Science,* edited by Watson Davis. Reprinted by permission of the director, Science Service Inc.

Charles Scribner's Sons, Publishers, for the quotation from *The Earth Speaks to Bryan,* by Henry Fairfield Osborn (1925). —And for the quotation from *Biography of the Unborn,* by Margaret Shea Gilbert (1932).

Simon and Schuster, for quotations from *The Story of Philosophy,* rev. ed. (1933), by Will Durant.

The Theosophical Publishing House, for quotations from *The Bhagavad-Gita,* translated by Annie Besant; published by The Theosophical Press, 1929.

Time, Inc., for the quotation from "The Universe According to Hoyle," which appeared in *Time* on November 20, 1950 (reprinted in *The Reader's Digest,* March, 1951).

The Viking Press, Inc., for the quotation from the Introduction to *The Bible of the World,* edited by Robert O. Ballou. Copyright 1939 by Robert O. Ballou. All rights reserved.

(Note: The quotations from Kenneth Hayes Miller are taken from the *Art Students League News,* Vol. 5, No. 2, and Vol. 6, No. 8.)

SEARCHING FOR THE TRUTH

ACCOMPLISHMENT

The plan is man's. The accomplishment is up to the heavens.

Chinese Proverb

Most often man's mission is against his personal inclinations. Seldom is anything considerable achieved unless there is this tension between desire and duty.

The World in the Making
COUNT HERMANN KEYSERLING

In the one thing done well, is a symbol of everything that is well done.

JOHANN WOLFGANG VON GOETHE

It is only the inadequate which is productive.

JOHANN WOLFGANG VON GOETHE

ACTION

One might suppose, what in fact all Philistines imagine, that the actions of a godly man must always appear good to everyone, but this is not true or possible. It might be possible if everyone were as profound, as inward as he, but as this assumption is not correct, his actions are often judged by others as blameworthy, a fact which is amply proved by the habitual persecution of the spiritual great.

The Travel Diary of a Philosopher
COUNT HERMANN KEYSERLING

By performing action without attachment, man verily reacheth the Supreme.

The Bhagavad-Gita (Hindu Scriptures)
The Bible of the World

Better to light one candle than to curse the darkness.

The Christophers' Motto

ADJUSTMENT

Everyone is inevitably onesided, since no one is equally apt in all things, and every light throws its correlative shadow. But he who correctly recognizes his limitations, and so adjusts himself, that he works only on the basis of those advantages which are an actual part of him, bears the same relation to the totality of humanity, as the eye does to the totality of the body, and he actually cannot help producing what is valid and profitable to all.

The World in the Making
COUNT HERMANN KEYSERLING

ADVENTURE

When we believe and "feel" ourselves to be adventurers . . . we become invulnerable.

The Challenge of Change
G. A. R. WYLIE

Goethe's constant aim was to be a living example of how a man could be adventurous, without being eccentric.

Goethe: The History of a Man
EMIL LUDWIG

AGE

True understanding teaches that we must recognize and grant to every stage of life all the value it can possibly have. Nothing is lovelier than genuine childhood, as long as it lasts. Nothing is more charming than youth pursuing its ends within a proper frame. But those spiritual experiences which lead to the realization of the meaning of life (the only thing capable of satisfying our deeps) begin as a rule with middle age, and old age alone creates that inner distance between the accidents and the innermost meaning of life, which makes it possible to understand it thoroughly, and to master it.

Problems of Personal Life
COUNT HERMANN KEYSERLING

The normal age of a man who lives rightly should be one hundred and forty; that is, seven times his maturity at twenty. But it is quite easy to double this span. There are many Mahatmas in the high Himalayas of over two hundred.

The Swami
Lancer at Large
FRANCIS YEATS-BROWN

Science has conferred on those people who have availed themselves of the newer knowledge of infectious diseases, better health, and greatest average length of life.

Dr. S. McLester, quoted in
"Vitamins for Everybody"
PAUL DE KRUIF
Reader's Digest, May 1941

The Butterfly wants not months but moments, and has time enough.

RABINDRANATH TAGORE

ANIMALS

The Lord Buddha taught kindness to animals as well as to men.

Lancer at Large
FRANCIS YEATS-BROWN

Elephants know music.

MRS. POWERS, *a former elephant trainer, speaking on the Bessie Beatty Radio Broadcast, 1941*

Like the dog in Jack London's great novel, man hesitates between "the call of the wild" and "the call of Man." The dog, in obeying the first, only abandons a sentimental servitude and follows the stronger voice of his ancestral instincts. He does not fall, he does not betray, because he has ceased to evolve. His destiny is to be a dog. . . . When man hesitates . . . If he possesses the sense of good and evil, and deliberately chooses evil, he betrays.

Human Destiny
LECOMTE DU NOÜY

The animal can measure in two directions only—it can never measure in three directions at once. This is due to the fact that, not possessing concepts, it is unable to retain in the mind the idea of the first two directions, for measuring the third. . . . This is deduced from the fact that they have no speech.

Tertium Organum
P. D. OUSPENSKY

Instinct, i.e., the ability developed by millenniums of selection, to act expediently without consciousness of purpose.

Tertium Organum
P. D. OUSPENSKY

The animal is conscious through his sensations and emotions. The intellect is present in the animal only in an embryonic state, as an emotion of curiosity, and pleasure of knowing.

Tertium Organum
P. D. Ouspensky

I have mentioned the apparent sense of the homing pigeon. That this is telepathic is evidenced by pigeons in flight. They automatically form groups that wheel, rise and settle, all in one accord.

What's on Your Mind?
Joseph Dunninger

The master does not allow any harm to be wrought to any living creatures. . . . The mechanic Zoroaster da Peretola has told me that Leonardo ever since his youthful years does not eat meat . . . and says there will come a time when all men, like him, will be content with vegetarian fare, deeming the killing of animals just as criminal as the killing of men . . .

We create our life out of the deaths of others! Men and beasts are but the eternal resting places of the dead, the graves for one another. . . .

Nature finding endless joy in the invention of new forms, in the building of new lives, and creating them with a greater speed than time can exterminate, has contrived so that certain creatures, nourishing themselves on others, may clear the space for coming generations. That is why she not infrequently sends plagues wherever creatures have multiplied excessively, especially men, with whom the excess of births is not balanced by deaths, inasmuch as the other beasts do not devour them.

Thus does Leonardo—though with great calmness of reason—explain natural laws, without waxing indignant or lamenting; but he himself acts in accordance with another law, abstaining from using as food anything that hath life within it.

The Romance of Leonardo da Vinci
DMITRI MEREJKOWSKI

I started singing softly to myself in a monotone; that is the best way to lull fear, and to establish friendly relationship with any animal.

Scent of Fear
JACK MELVILLE

Some vivisection experiments and gland-grafting operations inspire me with horror and revulsion. So do all circus performances with wild animals, because they are so pointless and unnecessary. But the matter is one of degree. The plain fact remains that man cannot exist on the earth without inflicting suffering on other parts of creation. . . . So in spite of my sorrow . . . I admit their necessity. . . . The Pasteur treatment generally effects a cure, although it is by no means infallible.

Lancer at Large
FRANCIS YEATS-BROWN

ARCHITECTURE

The Parthenon in Greece was deliberately built without symmetrical lines, which gives it magic.

JOHN GUNTHER
TV, July 2, 1960

ART

The "man of science" does not recognize the difference in the quality of the energy spent by two men going, one to his work, and another to denounce someone. For the man of science this difference is negligible: . . . . But perhaps the difference is much deeper and consists not in the difference in modes of energy but in the difference in men, one of whom is able to develop energy of one sort and another that of a different sort. Now here we have a form of knowledge which senses this difference perfectly, knows and understands it. I am speaking of art.

Tertium Organum
P. D. OUSPENSKY

The interpretation of emotional feelings and emotional understanding, is the problem of art. In combinations of words, in their meaning, their rhythm, their music—the combination of meaning, rhythm and music; in sounds, colors, lines, forms—men are creating a new world, and are attempting therein to express and transmit that which they feel, but which they are unable to express and transmit simply in words, i.e., in concepts. . . . The combination of feeling and thought of high tension leads to a higher form of psychic life. Thus in art we have already the first experiments in a language of the future. Art anticipates a psychic evolution and divines its future forms.

Tertium Organum
P. D. OUSPENSKY

It is in the works of art that nations have deposited their profoundest intuitions and ideas of their hearts; and fine art is frequently the key—with many nations there is no other—to the understanding of their wisdom and their religion. Yes, but why? Why in the fine arts rather than in the religions themselves, in the sciences and the philosophies, the civic structures, the political institutions, should we have the key to the human soul, the deepest strata of its intuitions, its innermost wisdom? For the simple reason, shall we not answer, that they speak the language of the soul, rather than the intellect, in a universal language, universally understood.

Hegel, quoted in
The Human Situation
W. MACNEILE DIXON

Art lives by reason of its function, which is to enable men to break free from their human condition, not by shirking it, but by an act of possession. All art is a means to gain hold on fate.

ANDRÉ MALRAUX

The art of dancing stands at the source of all the arts that express themselves first in the human person. The art of building, or architecture, is the beginning of all the arts that lie outside the person; and in the end they unite.

The Dance of Life
HAVELOCK ELLIS

The genuine artist, the tradition builder, strives for artistic truth: the other who only obeys a blind itch to create, strives for natural resemblance. Through the one, art is brought to its highest peak, and through the other its lowest depths.

JOHANN WOLFGANG VON GOETHE

The Peter Bell of poetry, the literalist (who is the lowest type) copies photographically what he sees and feels. He may arrange his material in the most pleasing of combinations, but the sensation to which he appeals, whether knowingly or not, is the Pleasure of Recognition. His great ideal is to heighten the individual object or experience to its most beautiful or most typical form.

William Blake: His Philosophy and Symbols
S. FOSTER DAMON

I began to realize at last the important truth, that I, or any other writer or artist, must always remain a humble servant and never assume the part of arrogant master. The prancing army was not me. I was only the one who patiently built the road over which it might ride.

Journals and Letters of the Little Locksmith
KATHARINE BUTLER HATHAWAY

Poetry, we are told, is for solace. It is only a way of escape. It is aside from life's realities. This nonsense is still repeated, though the truth is that when a civilization goes the way of all flesh, its energy survives in its books, art, science, and architecture.

The Wind Is Rising
H. M. TOMLINSON

The artist is a medium.

COUNT HERMANN KEYSERLING

Art is by its nature a secondary expression of culture; only philosophers, statesmen, and founders of religions are builders of culture. Let him who labors under the delusion of art as a creator of culture only recall this, that the artist is feminine in his nature, creates only under stimulus or because of somebody; so much so indeed, that it is often difficult to say whose share in the production of a great work of art is greater, that of the artist or that of the patron.

The World in the Making
Count Hermann Keyserling

Design is the greatest talent; genius, virtuosity in painting, are as nothing, compared with the talent for design. Renoir would have been a greater painter if he had had Daumier's sense of design.

Kenneth Hayes Miller

One thinks of the materials we work in as being unyielding and obdurate. It is not so; it is the mind that is obdurate and unyielding.

Kenneth Hayes Miller

Nature will not give us an art form. People spend a lifetime thinking they can get a form from nature to put on canvas. It isn't in nature. We get art from art. The canvas is the only reality. If the thing you take your painting from is the reality, your painting is second rate.

Kenneth Hayes Miller

The relation of art to nature is akin to metaphor. Art aims to render the character in terms of something else; in terms of canvas and paint. In these transformations, these masterly illusions, the subjective powers are not limited by what is limited.

Kenneth Hayes Miller

The wonderful thing about a painting is not that it looks like the model, but that it doesn't.

Kenneth Hayes Miller

What Miller called "Art Form" was his primary concern in painting. He believed that it is that element of a good picture which exists independently of representation.

KENNETH HAYES MILLER

The one quality which deserves to be rewarded with renown in art, is courage; a form of courage of which the common herd has no idea.

The Poor Relations
HONORÉ DE BALZAC

If I were to start to tell you of the shoulderblades or the clavicle and how the muscles are set upon it, you would all gather round and listen. . . . These are not important. But the big things are not to be taken for granted. . . . How striking to see a man running! . . . The torso becomes separated into legs. And the arms with their ability to turn in again on the figure and make the interesting spaces between. These are the things that are not to be taken for granted, but expressed.

KENNETH HAYES MILLER

Modern art seems to express despairing mockery. Art that goes after effects is dissolving, dying, in a state of decadence. Art that concerns itself with objects, with actualities of forms, is concerned with life.

KENNETH HAYES MILLER

The only way we have gained knowledge of ourselves, or have brought anything to the surface and to our own understanding of what we are, is by experience with the forms of our own environment in their congruous and familiar identity.

KENNETH HAYES MILLER

Space cannot be excluded from our plastic concepts; it is defined by the form itself, in our attitude toward it.

Line is an aspect of form, perhaps not inherent in it, but taken rather as a mode of sensing it, as a gesture imitating its contour or motion.

It is a serious modification of form if no back or reverse view is provided.

KENNETH HAYES MILLER

Ryder felt the conjunction of two forms, or the passing of one before the other, with the intensity which transformed casual positions of things into events of dramatic power.

KENNETH HAYES MILLER

Contrasts within the form should not be greater than around the form. Don't ever put modeling on modeling. Don't look at things with your hands behind your back. That's what form is in painting: An appetite for grasping.

Emotion in art is suspect because it tends to displace some of the form.

KENNETH HAYES MILLER

Competition, rivalries, calumnies, are the destroyers of talent. (In art.)

The Girl With the Golden Eyes
HONORÉ DE BALZAC

The two great qualities which art requires for its inception, are earnestness and detachment.

In the Introduction to
Miguel de Unamuno's
"The Tragic Sense of Life"
SALVADOR DE MADARIAGA

At the present stage of our development we possess nothing so powerful, as an instrument of knowledge of the world of causes, as art.

Tertium Organum
P. D. Ouspensky

The sun is neither moral or immoral. It is that which is. It lightens the darkness of space. And so does art.

Romain Rolland

Art is a powerful instrument of knowledge of the noumenal world: mysterious depths, each one more amazing than the last, open to the vision of man when he holds in his hands this magical key. But let him only think that this mystery is not for knowledge but for pleasure in it, and all the charm disappears at once. Just as soon as art begins to take delight in that beauty which is already found, instead of the search for new beauty an arrestment occurs and art becomes a superfluous estheticism, encompassing man's vision like a wall. The aim of art is the search for beauty.

Tertium Organum
P. D. Ouspensky

There cannot be a great art today however numerous the talents which are born and trained; for *art* as *an expression of the essential* presupposes an existing culture.

The World in the Making
Count Hermann Keyserling

BALANCE

Each given state of balance renders possible a higher development of certain activities, while precluding an equally high development of others.

America Set Free
Count Hermann Keyserling

BEAUTY

The beautiful is a manifestation of the secret laws of nature, which without its presence would never have been revealed.

JOHANN WOLFGANG VON GOETHE

Beauty knows to say enough. Barbarism clamors for still more.

RABINDRANATH TAGORE

BENEVOLENCE

Profuse benevolence of the rich are as nothing compared with the example of lives inspired by the imagination which conceives in its reality the unity of the race, and the wholeness of human life.

WILLIAM BLAKE

Behold I do not give lectures or a little charity. When I give I give myself.

WALT WHITMAN

It can only be conveyed by a certain grand manner which may be called good manners. . . . It cannot be done by giving gold or even bread; for it is a proverb that any reveller may fling largesses in mere scorn. It cannot even be done by giving time and attention; for any number of philanthropists and benevolent bureaucrats do such work with a scorn far more cold and horrible in their hearts. No plans or proposals or efficient rearrangements will give back to a broken man his self-respect and sense of speaking with an equal. One gesture will do it.

St. Francis of Assisi
GILBERT CHESTERTON

BEST

The highest authorities, and our own intuitions, teach us that we will make no mistake in living up to the best that is in us, so far as is possible.

The Kabalion
HERMES TRISMEGISTUS
Ancient Hermetic Philosophy, Egyptian and Greek

BODY

Our bodies, like those of various plants and animals, are composed of cells. We are one and all, constellations, cellular communities. There are within these communities brain cells, and liver cells and stomach cells, each variety engaged upon its own separate task, yet all working in harmony to keep the body healthy and alive.

The Human Situation
W. MACNEILE DIXON

For ants, the different varieties of cells, with their separate tasks, are not enclosed in one body, but are separate individuals.

NOYES
(*Paraphrase*)

The germ cell is a unit and does not become specialized for the production of the heart or lungs, or any other part of the body till it has attained a certain maturity. If at an early stage it be divided, or subjected to pressure, or even if a portion be removed, the germ retains its powers. It possesses the astonishing faculty of providing any necessary organ out of any part of itself. Utterly unlike any machine, the cells, too, in living things can act for each other, and work together for a common purpose. This co-operation of parts is everywhere present in natural organisms.

The Human Situation
W. MACNEILE DIXON

By the end of the month, the embryo (of the human being) is about one-fourth of an inch long, curled almost in a circle, with a short pointed tail below his belly, and small nubbins either side of his body are incipient arms and legs. On the sides of his short neck appear four clefts, comparable to the gill-slits of a fish, another "evolutionary hangover."

Biography of the Unborn
MARGARET SHEA GILBERT

BONDAGE

The freedom of the storm
And the bondage of the stem
Join hands in the dance
Of the swaying branches.

RABINDRANATH TAGORE

The further the creation from the center, the more it is bound.

The Kabalion
HERMES TRISMEGISTUS

The wise men of Gothem thought to preserve eternal summer by building a wall about the cuckoo, and were surprised to find the bird dead in the winter snows.

The Challenge of Change
G. A. R. WYLIE

CAUTION

When you find that prudent people do not commend you, adhere to your own act, and congratulate yourself that you have done something strange and extravagant: Give your heart a holiday from caution.

RALPH WALDO EMERSON

CHANGE

No man must have a fixed ideal enthroned in the sculptured beauty of dead marble. That is death. The ideal must change with each rising step of consciousness, and none must fear to deny his former convictions, or to follow where the new lead him. That they may lead him into strange and difficult places I do not deny, but he will walk in the midst of fire unharmed.

The House of Fulfilment
L. ADAMS BECK

There are no static things or objects, located in fixed positions. All is process, movements, events, some slow on our scale, like the drift of continents, some fast like radiation.

The Human Situation
W. MACNEILE DIXON

Like all true innovators and unlike those whose bloodless, intellectual productions aim at overthrowing the great traditions in art, Sibelius believes that the new and transforming ideas must come from within, not from the exterior form.

Sibelius
BENGT DE TÖRNE

CHARACTER

Character: [the possession of] high qualities [of] moral force.

Funk and Wagnalls Practical Standard Dictionary

The value of any experience of any idea, is its tendency in the way of making character.

In the Hours of Meditation
F. J. ALEXANDER

So of the rest of our actions: (character) . . . runs as straight as a ruled line through them all, no matter how many curvets about it. Our whole life is taxed for the least thing well done; it is the net result. How we eat, drink, sleep and use our desultory hours, now in these indifferent days with no eye to observe and no occasion to excite us, determines our authority and capacity for the time to come.

Thoreau's Journal, Feb. 28, 1841
HENRY DAVID THOREAU

Life plants no seeds in a man but the sun and the snow of the years both quicken and kill what seeds were in him at his birth, and thus the main trunk of character grows.

The Seven Ages of Washington
OWEN WISTER

CHRISTIANITY

Why was it that Jesus exalted the weary and the heavy laden, the unimportant and the silent in the land? Because He had in mind only the introvert; He had to do this, for His Kingdom was not of this world. The introvert is actually adapted to external life only in the form of humility; his structure being what it is, he cannot conquer life. But for that very same reason he must not set the tone for this world. He may do it for the beyond—à chacun so tour—but in this world he is subordinate to the one who radiates life out of himself. The type of the latter alone can give body to the highest conceptions of man.

Europe
COUNT HERMANN KEYSERLING

What the western world is really made for is, indeed, not the Christian age, but the age of the Holy Ghost. The western race being all too worldly-minded by instinct, they badly needed an education inspired by a fundamentally unworldly spirit (Christ); and it is very fortunate it fell to their share. Since the emancipation of the intellect however, the West has started on its own peculiar road. As yet it is groping, by many ways and byways, for a light visualized somewhere far off; in the heavens, in the past, in the future, but which really shines within the soul of each.

America Set Free
COUNT HERMANN KEYSERLING

The whole tenor of Christ's life tells me beyond possibility of personal doubt, that the Divinity that descended on Him, other men may also attain.

Lancer at Large
FRANCIS YEATS-BROWN

To its eternal honor Christianity has stood steadfastly for the sanctity of the individual. To imprison the human spirit is the unpardonable sin, the attempt to make men automata, to force them into the same mold. No means will ever be found to induce human beings finally to surrender themselves, either body or soul, to a dictated felicity, to satisfactions chosen for them, whatever vulgar Caesars rule the world. And upon this rock all forms of regimentation, of standardized existence will eventually shipwreck.

The Human Situation
W. MACNEILE DIXON

CONFORMITY

The virtue in most request is conformity. Whoso would be a man, must be a non-conformist.

RALPH WALDO EMERSON

CONSCIENCE

Nobody has the right to substitute his own conscience for that of another, for progress depends on personal effort, and to suppress this effort constitutes a crime.

Human Destiny
LECOMTE DU NOÜY

CONSISTENCY

Consistency is the hobgoblin of weak minds.

RALPH WALDO EMERSON

CONTRAST

Truly to enjoy bodily warmth, some part of you must be cold, for there is no quality in this world that is not what it is merely by contrast; nothing exists in itself.

Moby Dick
HERMAN MELVILLE

CORRESPONDENCE

The principal of correspondence: As above so below; as below so above.

The Kabalion
HERMES TRISMEGISTUS

The objects I behold correspond to my mood.

Thoreau's Journal
HENRY DAVID THOREAU

As our planet revolves every year around the sun, and at the same time turns once in every twenty-four hours upon its axis, thus traversing minor cycles within a larger one, so is the work of the smaller cyclic periods accomplished and recommenced. . . . The revolution of the physical world, according to ancient doctrine, is attended by a like revolution in the world of the intellect—the spiritual evolution of the world proceeding in cycles like the physical one. As above, so below. That which has been will return again. As in heaven, so on earth.

Isis Unveiled
H. P. BLAVATSKY

The glittering of the sun in the brushwood is as a myriad of tiny yellow stars.

Rodin's Diary
FRANÇOIS AUGUSTE RODIN

COSMIC

From the depths of space, from the furthest stars, influences pour down upon us, as in cosmic radiation—from sources at which we can but dimly guess.

The Human Situation
W. MACNEILE DIXON

To get the scale of cosmic things, we must perceive nature for what she is, as everlastingly and furiously dynamic, permitting nothing throughout her whole circumference to be at rest, not for so much as a moment.

The Human Situation
W. MACNEILE DIXON

The distinguishing signs of those men in whom cosmic consciousness is likely to manifest are not studied at all.

The first of these signs is the constant or frequent sensation that the world is not at all as it appears; that what is most important in it is not at all what is considered most important. . . .

High mental culture, high intellectual attainments, are not necessary conditions at all. The example of many saints, who were not intellectual, but who undoubtedly attained cosmic consciousness, shows that cosmic consciousness may develop in purely emotional soil, i.e., in the given case as a result of religious emotion. Cosmic consciousness is also possible of attainment through the emotion attendant upon creation—in painters, musicians and poets. Art in its highest manifestations is a path to cosmic consciousness.

But equally in all cases the unfoldment of cosmic consciousness demands a certain culture, a correspondent life. From all the examples cited by Dr. Bucke, and all that one might add, it would not be possible to select a single case in which cosmic consciousness unfolded in conditions of inner life adverse to it, i.e., in moments of absorption by the outer life, with its struggles, its emotions and interests.

For the manifestation of cosmic consciousness it is necessary that the center of gravity of everything shall lie for man in the inner world, in self-consciousness, and not in the outer world at all. . . .

This conclusion in regard for special culture and definitely favorable inner and outer conditions, does not necessarily mean that cosmic consciousness is likely to manifest in every man who is put in these conditions. There are men, probably an enormous majority of contemporary humanity, in whom exists no such possibility at all. And in those who do not possess it in some sort already, it cannot be created by any culture whatever, in the same way that no kind or amount of culture will make an animal speak the language of man. The possibility of the manifestation of cosmic consciousness cannot be inoculated artificially. A man is either born with it or born without it. This possibility can be throttled or developed, but it cannot be created.

Tertium Organum
P. D. OUSPENSKY

COURAGE

Courage comes from thought. Bravery is often impatience at danger.

Napoleon
ELIE FAURE

CREATION

As a spider spins out his web from within himself and draws it in at pleasure; or as herbs grow out of the earth; or as hair grows out of the living man, so indeed, does evolve the Kosmos from the ever immutable one.

Mundaka
Indian Philosophy and Modern Culture
PAUL BRUNTON

Reason and intellect are not endowed with creativeness. . . . Nobody has ever created anything unless he has been moved and stirred to the very bottom of his soul. And man can only be so moved and stirred according to the law of polarization, by means of that force which is love in its widest sense.

Problems of Personal Life
COUNT HERMANN KEYSERLING

Every search for new harmonic tissue, every pursuit of unknown orchestral color, be it systematic or improvised and spontaneous, should remain subordinate to the imagination of the artist. Only thus would the composer preserve his spiritual independence, his individuality; only thus would his conceptions assume the character of a work of art, being the true expression of ideas suggested to the author, by his inspiration, supported by solid technical knowledge and experience.

Sibelius
BENGT DE TÖRNE

A man can create life values only with the thoughts which bespeak him personally. These thoughts are undoubtedly his whether they have occurred to him or whether he adopted them; for to discover and to understand are metaphysically one.

The World in the Making
COUNT HERMANN KEYSERLING

No man is the master of any productive energy; and all men must let it work on by itself.

Life and Character
JOHANN WOLFGANG VON GOETHE

We know that nothing can be lost. If energy exists, then it must transform itself into something. Now if a merely negligible percentage of energy goes into the creation of the future by begetting, then the remainder must go into the creation of the future also, but in another way. We have in the physical world many cases in which the direct function is effected by a very small percentage of the consumed energy, and the greater part is spent without return, as it were.

But of course this greater part of energy does not disappear, is not wasted, but accomplishes other results quite different from the direct function.

Tertium Organum
P. D. Ouspensky

The themes of musical ideas of your youth are the richest and best you will ever invent, and even if you cannot give them at once their definite shape, they will later on form the basis of some of your happiest conceptions.

Sibelius
Bengt de Törne

In writing, Sibelius certainly did not think of creating something new; he simply listened to his irresistible, volcanic inspiration and accepted its direction.

Sibelius
Bengt de Törne

No advice, however great, can save a composer if he has no intrinsic value.

Sibelius
Bengt de Törne

The ideal of creativeness is the only one which can become the general ideal of future humanity, either free or anxious to free itself, from the material and moral fetters forged by mechanization.

Problems of Personal Life
Count Hermann Keyserling

CRIME

Crime is a state of mind, whether it be in the most crowded tenement districts or in the broad expanse of meadows and brooks and beautiful vistas.

Persons in Hiding
J. EDGAR HOOVER

There is nothing mysterious about crime—the germ of crime is universal. Criminality has its sources in the human impulses of mankind, which are neither good nor bad in themselves, but are so only in relation to other things.

Life and Death in Sing Sing
EX-WARDEN LEWIS E. LAWES

Neither poverty or wealth is the cause of any crime, but under certain circumstances either may become a dominant factor.

Life and Death in Sing Sing
EX-WARDEN LEWIS E. LAWES

It is not the terror of brutal punishment that holds the units of society in their place. It is customs and habits.

Story of My Life
CLARENCE DARROW

Criminals lack imagination.

"'Real Life Sherlock' From Criminal Record Office"
TONY HOWARD
(Saturday Evening Post, October 28, 1961)

The only thing necessary for crime to triumph is for good men to do nothing about it.

EDMUND BURKE

Most prisoners resent pity or sympathy and have no use for reformers of any kind. . . . All they ask of anybody is a square deal right down the line.

Life and Death in Sing Sing
EX-WARDEN LEWIS E. LAWES

Imprisonment is itself punishment.

Life and Death in Sing Sing
EX-WARDEN LEWIS E. LAWES

The assumption that a person perversely wills, without rhyme or reason, to do wrong in preference to right, is ridiculous in the extreme.

Life and Death in Sing Sing
EX-WARDEN LEWIS E. LAWES

The death penalty originated among primitive savages, by whom it was used to remove the unfit; that is, the deformed, crippled, insane, aged, and others including the over-fat who hampered the family tribe in its activities.

Life and Death in Sing Sing
EX-WARDEN LEWIS E. LAWES

The broad effects which can be obtained by punishment in man and beast, are the increase of fear, the sharpening of the sense of cunning, the mastery of desires; so it is that punishment tames man, but does not make him better.

FRIEDRICH WILHELM NIETZSCHE

Responsibility must, in most instances, be shared by society which takes credit for man's virtues, and should (also) . . . acknowledge some of the blame for his vices.

Life and Death in Sing Sing
EX-WARDEN LEWIS E. LAWES

CRITICISM

Wise people do not contend against the tongues of fools.

Japanese Proverb

Against criticism a man can neither protest nor defend himself; he must act in spite of it, and then criticism will gradually yield to him.

Life and Character
Johann Wolfgang von Goethe

CULTURE

Culture is life form as direct expression of spirit.

The World in the Making
Count Hermann Keyserling

The more we think, the higher we get in development, the harder it is to coordinate, and finally balance the different sides of ourselves, to live from the inner man; but this is what culture really means.

Lecture
Count Hermann Keyserling

Every true state of culture is consciously based on tradition on the one hand, and on the other feels responsible for the future as an integral part of itself.

America Set Free
Count Hermann Keyserling

Any man can stand a life in the wilds, this being the normal kind of life for the human animal, but only the traditional culture makes man fit to stand cultural surroundings.

America Set Free
Count Hermann Keyserling

Family culture and family culture alone can create that hatching warmth and that atmosphere favorable to growth which the soul needs.

Problems of Personal Life
COUNT HERMANN KEYSERLING

Culture is always a daughter of spirit married to earth.

America Set Free
COUNT HERMANN KEYSERLING

The death of the old culture as a consequence of the development of the intelligence is a case of real destiny, for it imparts nothing less than the displacement of the earlier type of man by a more recent one which because of its special aptitude is unable to continue the old.

The World in the Making
COUNT HERMANN KEYSERLING

DARING

The great man has never been in the habit of leaving the conduct of things to the Almighty, as the general run of believers in destiny believe. The great man has always known exactly, that the cosmic dispensation expresses itself in free decision precisely through the instrumentality of his daring.

The World in the Making
COUNT HERMANN KEYSERLING

I leaped headlong into the sea, and thereby have become better acquainted with the soundings, the quicksands and the rocks than if I had stayed upon the green shore, and piped a silly pipe, and took tea and comfortable advice.

JOHN KEATS

DEATH

Death [is] not a call to annihilation. . . . It is the extinction of the lamp in the morning light; not the abolition of the sun.

Sadhana
Rabindranath Tagore

It is really courting death when we refuse to accept death; when we wish to give the form of the self some fixed changelessness; when the self feels no impulse which urges it to grow out of itself; when it treats its limits as final, and acts accordingly.

Sadhana
Rabindranath Tagore

Nothing is born and nothing dies; it only so represents itself to us, because we see but the sections of things. In reality, the circle of life is only the section of something, and that something undoubtedly exists before birth, i.e., before the appearance of the circle in our space, and continues to exist after death, i.e., after the disappearance of the circle from the field of our vision.

Tertium Organum
P. D. Ouspensky

The personality must be sacrificed. Who am I to think that my little self shall continue immortal when I know that creation is dissolving at various rates under the relentless march of time? Yet there is no death, and no loss in the Vedanta, for I am the world. I am the dawn, the dew, the wind, the rain, the sun at noon-day, the tenderness of evening, the sea, the sky, the mountain, humanity, the lover and the loved, the known and the knowing. I have renounced my little straying personality for the Universal Cosmic Consciousness.

Vedanta philosophy, from
Lancer at Large
FRANCIS YEATS-BROWN

DEMOCRACY

True democracy is not that which levels everything, but that which makes possible for each man his complete development. It is not a question of political, but of spiritual democracy.

Problems of Personal Life
COUNT HERMANN KEYSERLING

True superiority has always been due to chance and accidents in blood mixtures of whose laws we are entirely ignorant; hence the absolute surprise which true genius always means; hence the scarcity of families and races of lasting superiority. All this pleads for democratization and not for eugenics as at least the first forward step to be taken.

Problems of Personal Life
COUNT HERMANN KEYSERLING

DEPRESSION

Take depression for granted. One who expects completely to escape low moods is asking for the impossible. To take low moods too seriously, instead of saying "This will pass," is to confer on them an obsessive power they need not have.

On Being a Real Person
HARRY EMERSON FOSDICK

DEPTH

The greatest rivers flow under ground.

The Romance of Leonardo da Vinci
Dmitri Merejkowski

DESIRE

Men obtain only a portion of that which they desire.

Notes on the Bhagavad-Gita
William Judge *and* Robert Crosbie

DESPISING

Christ was despised by most men.

Author Unknown

DESTINY

Let every man remember that the destiny of mankind is incomparable and that it depends greatly on his will to collaborate in the transcendent task. Let him remember that the law is, and always has been, to struggle and that the fight has lost nothing of its violence by being transposed from the material onto the spiritual planes; let him remember that his own dignity, his nobility as a human being, must emerge from his efforts to liberate himself from his bondage and to obey his deepest aspirations. And let him above all never forget that the divine spark is in him, and that he is free to disregard it, to kill it, or to become closer to God by showing his eagerness to work with Him and for Him.

Human Destiny
Lecomte du Noüy

DEVIL

"He who wrestles with us," . . . . "Strengthens our nerves, and sharpens our skill." Our antagonist is our helper. Satan, if we understand matters aright, is the ally rather than the enemy of Michael.

EDMUND BURKE

He wrestled with the devil, as every man must to be worth calling a man.

St. Francis of Assisi
GILBERT K. CHESTERTON

DIFFERENCES

Would the Hindoos, as recognizers and beholders of the divine, have reached such a singularly high plane if they had been different as human beings? Would they have realized the one thing which is needful to salvation if they had been capable of giving expression to it in life? Probably not. The great moralist is typically amoral, because freedom from prejudice means freedom from inhibition; the man whose understanding is great, is typically lacking in character, because he cannot regard any manifestation as being absolutely the best one; conversely the great man of action is typically narrow minded.

The Travel Diary of a Philosopher
COUNT HERMANN KEYSERLING

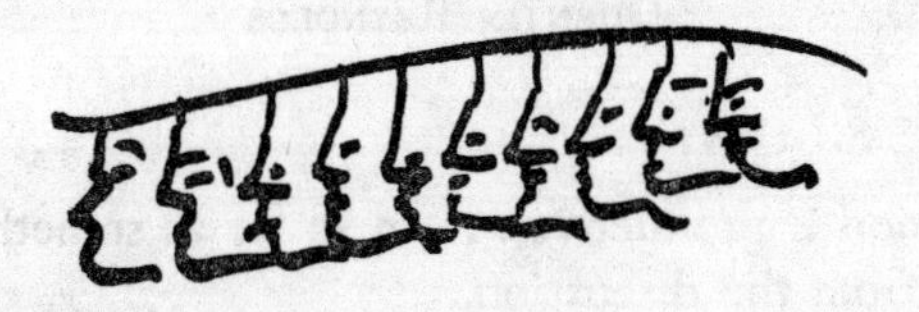

Ten men, ten minds.

Japanese Proverb

Men and women doubtless have different tasks on earth.

America Set Free
COUNT HERMANN KEYSERLING

If every day was a sunny day, who would not wish for rain?

Japanese Proverb

DISCIPLINE

Nothing is to me more important than, so far as is possible, to turn to the best account what is in me, and keep a firm hand on my idiosyncrasies.

JOHANN WOLFGANG VON GOETHE

DISCRIMINATION

I hope you will be able to choose between what is necessary in your life, and what is not necessary.

Mahant of Hatha Yogis
Lancer at Large
FRANCIS YEATS-BROWN

He who has a thing in hand to do, must know how to take sides.

JOHANN WOLFGANG VON GOETHE

Only the stars are neutral.

Title of a book by
QUENTIN REYNOLDS

DISCUSSION

Discussion is productive . . . in so far as something new originates from the discussion.

America Set Free
COUNT HERMANN KEYSERLING

One who can . . . oppose his ideas to mine . . . takes part in the conflict whence the light will spring, even as a spark is born of the concussion of two flints.

The Life of a Fly
JEAN HENRI FABRE

Every discussion is absolutely evil when one of the disputants fails to consider the other's point of view, or his opponent worthy of his respect, but rather assumes the incorrectness of an opinion or a position differing from his own.

America Set Free
COUNT HERMANN KEYSERLING

DISORGANIZATION

When the effect produced is no longer in direct relation or in equal proportions to the cause, disorganization begins.

César Birotteau
HONORÉ DE BALZAC

DRAMA

The truth is that this earth is the scene of a drama of which we only perceive scattered portions, and in which the greater number of the actors are invisible to us.

Mabel Collins, quoted in
Tertium Organum
P. D. OUSPENSKY

"Men must know," remarks Bacon, "that in the theatre of human life it is reserved for the gods and angels to be lookers on." To imagine ourselves angels, not to say gods, is a little difficult, but let us indulge the fancy that we are superior spectators of the world of drama, in the stalls and not on the stage, casually interested in the performance, but otherwise not concerned. What should we think of the play? We should, I conjecture, find it entertaining. We should praise the theatre, as an imposing edifice, and declare the scenery excellent, the plot intriguing and full of incident, the characters numerous and charmingly varied, the acting wonderfully realistic and convincing. To disapprove of the world as a spectacle would, we may agree, be hypercritical. As a passing show it leaves little to be desired, and is probably as well worth seeing as any other staged in the universe.

The Human Situation
W. Macneile Dixon

A workman is more effective and happy if he dramatizes himself as such . . . and all social relations can be given style, by a sense of the theatre.

R. F. D.
Charles Allen Smart

DRAWING

I think one imitates one's own body in drawing, because the soul is the artist of its body. At one time it had created and moulded it in its image and likeness, and now when it is again necessary it doth all the more willingly repeat the image in which it had once before become incarnate.

The Romance of Leonardo da Vinci
Dmitri Merejkowski

When I draw I do not know what I am going to make. I have no preconceived scheme in my mind. I take my pen and begin to draw, and suddenly I see a head, or a flower, or a cloud. . . . Sometimes I make mistakes. It is as if I broke the stem of a flower trying to bend it. Then the curve dies. I have led it on to its destruction. For all these little forms are like so many souls which expect their salvation from me.

RABINDRANATH TAGORE

DREAMS

[We] know that the events of today were the ideas and feelings of yesterday—and that the events of tomorrow are lying in someone's irritation, in someone's hunger, in someone's suffering, and probably still more in someone's imagination, in someone's fantasy, in someone's dreams.

Tertium Organum
P. D. OUSPENSKY

Modern mankind, with much hardship, often must relearn facts which were accepted by the ancients. . . . Now we are beginning to become aware of the possibility of dreams, in certain cases, accurately portraying future events.

DR. R. K. GREENBANK
Practicing psychiatrist
Florida Times-Union, September 13, 1964

Dreams are like flowers, and when they wither they become hay, and the oxen eat them.

Author Unknown

While we live we must live our dreams. There is no other way of passing beyond them into reality.

The Fountain
CHARLES MORGAN

If one advances confidently in the direction of his dreams, and endeavors to live the life he has imagined, he will meet with a success unexpected in common hours.

Walden
HENRY DAVID THOREAU

Christ and Napoleon lived their dreams instead of dreaming their lives.

Napoleon
ELIE FAURE

In waking life we are critical of the interpretive hypotheses that occur to us, and therefore do not make such wild mistakes as in dreams. But the creative as opposed to the critical mechanism is the same in the waking life as it is in dreams.

An Outline of Philosophy
LORD BERTRAND RUSSELL

Our dream images are composed of past and future experiences equally blended.

An Experiment With Time
J. W. DUNNE

EDUCATION

The educated criminal is probably more dangerous than the ignorant.

Life and Death in Sing Sing
EX-WARDEN LEWIS E. LAWES

The Brahmanical theory has also a far-reaching bearing on the problem of education. "Reading," says the Garuda Purana, "to a man devoid of wisdom, is like a mirror to the blind." The Brahmans attached no value to the uncoordinated knowledge or to unearned opinions, but rather regarded these as dangerous tools in the hands of unskilled craftsmen. The greatest stress is laid on the development of character.

The Dance of Siva
ANANDA COOMARASWAMY

The mind should be sharpened as a tool, not filled as a museum.

Author Unknown

The world's great men have not commonly been great scholars.

The Autocrat of the Breakfast Table
OLIVER WENDELL HOLMES

I could not tolerate the traditional methods of education which were employed in which individual traits and tendencies were ignored. One cannot grow a lily from the root of a cabbage, nor a cabbage from a lily root.

RABINDRANATH TAGORE

Our childhood should be given its full measure of life's draught, for which it has an endless thirst. The young mind should be saturated with the idea that it has been born in a human world which is in harmony with the world around it. This is just what our regular type of school ignores, with an air of superior wisdom. My feeling at school was the feeling of a tree that is not allowed its full life, but is cut down to be made into packing cases. My world vanished, giving place to wooden benches and straight walls staring at me with the blank stare of the blind. . . .

The education of sympathy is not only systematically ignored in schools but is severely repressed. We rob the child of his earth to teach him geography, of language to teach him grammar. His hunger is for the epic, but he is supplied with chronicles of facts and dates.

RABINDRANATH TAGORE

Boys and girls learn the "three R's" by keeping records of their marketing, make the acquaintance of geology on their own plot of ground, and of chemistry by using limes and manures. Nature and science are not abstractions: the child learns physics by using tools and pumps, and entomology by thwarting the mosquitoes, caterpillars, and beetles that attack him and his plants. Masters and pupils are engaged together in the adventure of life; both are learners in the game, and the emphasis is on the expanding of consciousness rather than on passing examinations. The world is their guitar, and it is no use having a guitar unless you play on it.

"Tagore's School in India"
Lancer at Large
FRANCIS YEATS-BROWN

I find nothing that excuses school boards who put up new buildings and believe that mortar, stone and steel make an education.

CHARLES E. BOEHM
Pennsylvania Superintendent of Public Instruction
Saturday Evening Post, May 14, 1960

Kindergarten and school represent the best of social influences, the home, or rather the right kind of home, . . . develops the individual tendencies and thus lays the foundation for the personality. The influence of kindergarten leads to nothing but socialization.

America Set Free
COUNT HERMANN KEYSERLING

There is a time in . . . man's education when he arrives at the conviction that envy is ignorance; that imitation is suicide; that he must take himself for better, for worse, as his portion.

RALPH WALDO EMERSON

More than to institute the process of self discovery of his way to another, and to hasten that process, lies beyond the power of any teacher.

COUNT HERMANN KEYSERLING

To the pupil belongs the honor of interpreting great works of art in the eye of the enraptured public. The master works in comparative obscurity, but works in the plastic material of life itself. "Professor Auer," said Max Rosen, "looks first for the nucleus of whatever ability each pupil possesses." While searching for "this hidden seed," he was gentle and tender, but when he had found it his grasp never relaxed. Refraining always from the attempt to force a youthful talent "beyond its highest level," he yet "forged it like a sword." One word was often on his lips: "First learn to sing." Of all instruments the violin is essentially vocal. Beyond that he has little or no method, except the method of an inspiration subtly felt and inerrantly controlled.

MAX ROSEN (*paraphrase*)

I think the better the composer, the worse the teacher.

Sibelius
BENGT DE TÖRNE

Mind itself becomes the Guru (teacher). This is an old teaching. And why? Because pressing in upon the mind for self-realization is the Divinity thou art.

In the Hours of Meditation
F. J. ALEXANDER

EFFORT

He who does not strive in effort, him I will not help on. He who does not knock . . . to him I will not open. He to whom I show one corner and he cannot transfer it to the other three, for him I will not repeat.

CONFUCIUS

A strenuous effort must be made by anyone who would escape from the tyranny of herd instinct.

ROMAIN ROLLAND

Somehow the crowd must be made to understand that the important thing is, not to follow but to make an individual effort.

Human Destiny
LECOMTE DU NOÜY

EMOTION

Personal emotion is always partial, always unjust, by reason of the one fact that it opposes itself to all the rest.

Thus the cognitive power of the emotions is greater in proportion as there is less of self-elements in a given emotion, i.e., more consciousness that this emotion is not the I.

Tertium Organum
P. D. OUSPENSKY

In the soul of man nothing exists save emotions. And the soul life of man is either a struggle or a harmonious adjustment between different emotions. Spinoza saw this quite clearly when he said that emotion can be mastered only by another more powerful emotion, and by nothing else.

Spinoza
Tertium Organum
P. D. OUSPENSKY

Christ driving the money-changers out of the temple, or expressing his opinion about the Pharisees, was not entirely meek and mild; and there are cases wherein meekness and mildness are not virtues at all. Emotions of love, sympathy, pity transform themselves very readily into sentimentality, into weakness; and thus transformed they contribute of course to nescience, i.e., matter. The difficulty of dividing emotions into categories is increased by the fact that all emotions of the higher order, without exception, can also be personal and then their action partakes of the nature of this class.

Tertium Organum
P. D. Ouspensky

EQUALITY

Men are not equal in capacity but in value.

Never Call Retreat
Joseph Freeman
Radio, March 19, 1943

Each and all should see in their personal life a sonata which must be properly played from beginning to end; whose every tempo, every phrase has its own special quality, where yet all phrased, in their diversity are necessary for the complete realization of the meaning in the composition, and whose end signifies both achievement, accomplishment and perfection. Once a man has understood this, he no longer claims that the scherzo is worth more than the adagio! In principle he recognizes in all tempos an equal value. The difference in value depends only upon the degree of realization of meaning which has been attained in each case.

Problems of Personal Life
Count Hermann Keyserling

ERROR

Error . . . is not sin but only youth.

ROMAIN ROLLAND
In the Introduction to
Ananda Coomaraswamy's
"The Dance of Siva"

ETERNITY

Drifting in a sultry day on the sluggish waters of the pond, I almost cease to live; and begin to be. A boatsman stretched on the deck of his craft and dallying with the noon would be as apt an emblem of eternity for me as the serpent with his tail in his mouth. I am never so prone to loose my identity. I am dissolved in the haze.

Thoreau's Journal, April 4, 1839
HENRY DAVID THOREAU

In the midst of our home and our work, the prayer rises, "Lead me across!" For here rolls the sea, and even here lies the other shore waiting to be reached—yes, here is the everlasting present, not distant, not anywhere else.

Sadhana
RABINDRANATH TAGORE

ETHICS

The great fault of all esthetes hitherto has been that they believed themselves to have to deal only with the relations of man to man. In reality however, the question is, what is his attitude to the world, and to all life that comes within his reach. A man is ethical only when life, as such, is sacred to him, that of plants and animals, as that of his fellow men.

ALBERT SCHWEITZER
Out of My Life and Thought

EVIL

The question of why there is evil in existence is the same as why there is imperfection, or, in other words, why there is creation at all. We must take it for granted that it could not be otherwise; that creation must be imperfect, must be gradual, and that it is futile to ask the question, Why we are?

But this is the real question we ought to ask: Is this imperfection the final truth; is evil absolute and ultimate? The river has its boundaries, its banks, but is a river all banks? Or are the banks the final facts about the river? Do not these obstructions themselves give its water an onward motion? The towing rope binds a boat, but is the bondage its meaning? Does it not at the same time draw the boat forward?

Sadhana
RABINDRANATH TAGORE

Evil perpetually tends to disappear.

HERBERT SPENCER

Evil is a necessity, if there is to be among the degrees of reality a world like ours, and our world such as it is, is in so far a manifestation of goodness and beauty, that its existence is preferable to its non-existence. For we have to remember that the question is not whether men and animals should be what they are, but whether they should be what they are or not at all.

The Human Situation
W. MACNEILE DIXON

EVOLUTION

The disciplined emotions are the keys to creative evolution.

Lancer at Large
FRANCIS YEATS-BROWN

We must throw overboard the whole idea of natural evolution. Such a thing does not exist. Nothing is less in agreement with facts and with meaning than Darwin's idea of life attaining a higher stage of development by way of natural progress. To start with, whoever says "natural" in science means "necessary," and a natural evolution of the lower toward the higher is certainly not necessary.

Problems of Personal Life
COUNT HERMANN KEYSERLING

EXAMPLE

I welcome always in my soul, the memory of the best and most renowned of men. Whenever the enforced associations of daily life arouse worthless, evil, or ignoble feelings, I am able to repel these feelings, and to keep them at a distance, by dispassionately turning my thoughts to contemplate the highest examples.

Preamble to the Life of Timoleon
PLUTARCH

Man by living from his inner self, can be an example to all humanity.

Lecture, January 26, 1928
COUNT HERMANN KEYSERLING

EXPRESSION

It is the very characteristic of life that it is not complete within itself; it must come out.

Sadhana
RABINDRANATH TAGORE

Each of us has something to express. . . . It is our sacred duty to find out what it is and work on it.

Polish Profile
VIRGILIA SAPIEHA

I fancy that the great men are rare (just as the fools are many) who have not at one time or another found their own external style, and then been true to it. The divine gift of vanity brought many a good thing in its wake. Anyone who has brought his costume and his nature into harmony, satisfies not only his personal and esthetic requirements, not only his consideration for his fellows—he has found in fact a means of expression for himself.

The Travel Diary of a Philosopher
COUNT HERMANN KEYSERLING

The most skillful hand can not convey what the mind has not experienced.

Chinese Art

Not that I advise you to aspire to fame. Your work should spring from a purer, simpler source. You should desire nothing more than to express your own thoughts, and to address yourself to the sympathy of those who are capable of thinking as you do. Fame follows those whom she is unworthy to guide.

Letter to Lord Byron
PERCY BYSSHE SHELLEY
(Quoted in "Ariel: The Life of Shelley" by André Maurois)

FACTS

The animal intelligence knows facts, the human mind has the power to apprehend truth.

Sadhana
RABINDRANATH TAGORE

FAITH

Be like the bird who pausing in her flight awhile, on
bough too slight,
Feels it give way beneath her and yet sings,
Knowing that she hath wings.

VICTOR HUGO

To: Those tens of thousands of my former wards who have justified my faith in human nature.

Life and Death in Sing Sing
(dedication page)
EX-WARDEN LEWIS E. LAWES

Works of men without faith in the world are like those wondrous shells that one finds upon the beach, from which the life that they enfolded has gone forever.

Chinese Art

Faith without works will not save us.

The Bhagavad-Gita (Hindu Scriptures)
The Bible of the World

The passion for reforming one's neighbors out of existence, or at least out of the existence they prefer—and the two are often found together—afflicts even more grievously those who have lost their faith in God than those who believe in Him.

The Human Situation
W. MACNEILE DIXON

FASHION

The fashions of this world are continuous change, and I would concern myself with things that are abiding.

JOHANN WOLFGANG VON GOETHE

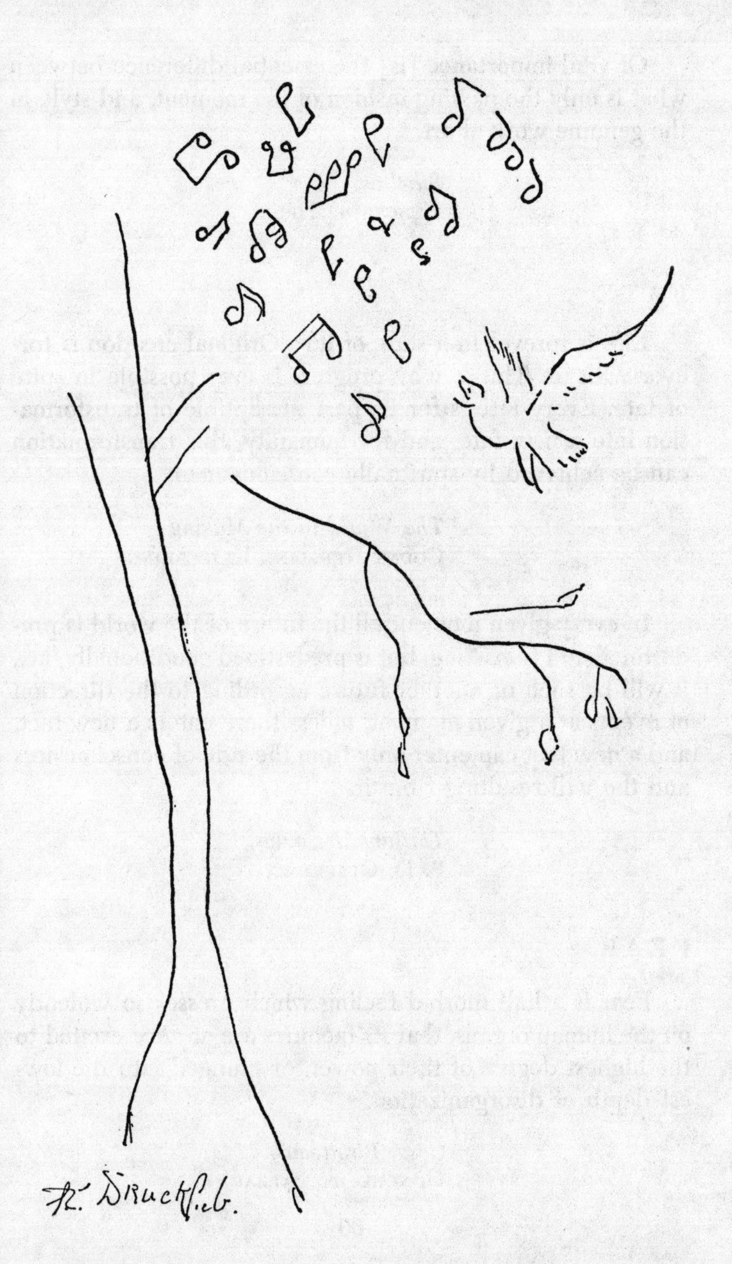

Of vital importance [is] the essential difference between what is only the passing fashion of the moment, and style in the genuine work of art.

Sibelius
Bengt de Törne

FATE

Life is forever in a state of flux. Original creation is forever with us. This is why progress is ever possible in spite of fate. Every fate is for its part susceptible of transformation into a new fate, and for humanity, this transformation can be achieved by spiritually conscious men.

The World in the Making
Count Hermann Keyserling

In every given moment all the future of the world is predestined and is existing, but is predestined conditionally, i.e., it will be such or another future according to the direction of events at a given moment, unless there enters a new fact, and a new fact can enter only from the side of consciousness and the will resulting from it.

Tertium Organum
P. D. Ouspensky

FEAR

Fear is a half morbid feeling which presses so violently on the human organs, that its faculties are at once excited to the highest degree of their power, or plunged into the lowest depth of disorganization.

César Birotteau
Honoré de Balzac

He who rides a tiger is afraid to dismount.

Chinese Proverb

The bird flying in the air does not fear the water.

Japanese Proverb

Reason cannot conquer feeling, because feeling can be conquered only by feeling. Reason can only give thoughts and pictures, evoking feelings which will conquer the feelings of a given moment.

Tertium Organum
P. D. OUSPENSKY

Don't be afraid. It's all here. Just lie back on it.

JOHN DEWEY

When I say that during most of my conscious life I have been a prey to fears, I take it for granted I am expressing the case of the majority of people.

Conquest of Fear
BASIL KING

Let then our first act every morning be to make the following resolve for the day:
I shall only fear God.
I shall not bear ill will toward anyone.
I shall not submit to injustice from anyone.
I shall conquer untruth by truth.
And in resisting untruth, I shall put up with all suffering.

MAHATMA GANDHI

FIGHTING

Buddha was one of the greatest of our Great Ones. But his philosophy has flaws. Harmlessness to all Creation: pacifism in excelsis, for instance. It is discussed in the Bhagavad-

Gita. Arjuna learns that he must fight for his principles, even sometimes for the right to live. That is the law which we cannot avoid.

Mahant of the Hatha Yogis
Lancer at Large
FRANCIS YEATS-BROWN

Only infants in reflection could suppose that the warfare in which, whether we like it or not, we never lay down the sword—not even the pacifist!—is the simple warfare between good and evil. Every good casts its dark shadow; every good is the enemy of another good.

The Human Situation
W. MACNEILE DIXON

FOOLS

A fool sees not the same tree that a wise man sees.

WILLIAM BLAKE

A fool shall not enter into heaven, let him be ever so holy.

William Blake: His Philosophy and Symbols
S. FOSTER DAMON

He who knows that he does not know, is never a fool.

Proverb

FORGIVENESS

Then said Jesus, Father, forgive them, for they know not what they do.

Luke 23:34

FREEDOM

The very foundation of the human organism is material, chemical, the same as that of animals. It must eat, sleep, procreate. It is difficult for man to evade this relationship, to free himself from the endocrine enslavement. By fighting against it he will affirm the difference to which he owes his human dignity, and by ceding to it he will abdicate the independence gained by hundreds of millions of years of evolution.

Human Destiny
LECOMTE DU NOÜY

When the harp is truly strung, when there is not the slightest laxity in the strength of the bond, then only does music result; and the string transcending itself in the melody, finds its every chord its true freedom. It is because it is bound, by such hard and fast rules on the one side, that it can find this range of freedom in music on the other. While the string was not true it was indeed merely bound; but a loosening of its bondage would not have been the way to freedom which it can only fully achieve by being bound tighter and tighter till it has attained the true pitch.

Sadhana
RABINDRANATH TAGORE

Inner freedom stands or falls by the will to run risks.

Europe
COUNT HERMANN KEYSERLING

The soul which is liberated . . . will be free from the desire to impose claims on others.

WILLIAM BLAKE

Man's freedom is never in being saved troubles, but it is the freedom to take trouble for his own good, to make the trouble an element of his joy.

Sadhana
RABINDRANATH TAGORE

He only earns his freedom, owns existence, who everyday must conquer her anew.

Faust
JOHANN WOLFGANG VON GOETHE

FUTURE

Whoever wishes to hasten the coming of a better future, should always start from the axiom that temporal conditions should be accepted as they are, and that one should embody in them the higher values one wishes to realize: Every idealist who fails to do so has wrong vision; he imagines that he can achieve success by using non-existent means.

Problems of Personal Life
COUNT HERMANN KEYSERLING

GENDER

The principle of gender is in everything; everything has its masculine and feminine principles. Law of gravitation, masculine principle, directs certain inherent energy toward feminine principle. Feminine does active creative work. Dual minds equals mental gender.

I am – Being.
Me – Becoming.
Masculine principal – will.

Feminine principle generates new thoughts, concepts, ideas including the work of the imagination.

The Kabalion
HERMES TRISMEGISTUS

GENEROSITY

Elementary wisdom . . . demands as a fundamental virtue generosity towards oneself and one's neighbor.

Problems of Personal Life
COUNT HERMANN KEYSERLING

GENIUS

Bain defines genius as the power of perceiving analogies.

Professor James quoted in
Tertium Organum
P. D. OUSPENSKY

Genius has always the child in his heart.

WILLIAM BLAKE

The activity of genius is not an obedience to rules but dedication of life, to what is commanded from within.

The Dance of Siva
ANANDA COOMARASWAMY

The social condition of genius is the same in all ages. Aeschylus was undoubtedly alone and without sympathy in his simple reverence for the mystery of the universe.

Thoreau's Journal, Jan. 29, 1840
HENRY DAVID THOREAU

The mob always rejoices in formulae; the genius usually tries to escape from them.

William Blake: His Philosophy and Symbols
S. FOSTER DAMON

GENUINE

He had been trying in a feeble way to be thorough in his work; he had not been thorough, the whole thing had been a fiasco; but he had made a little puny effort in the direction of being genuine, and behold in his hour of need it had been returned to him with a reward far richer than he had deserved.

The Way of All Flesh
SAMUEL BUTLER

GOD

That there is a source of life, a ground of things, sufficient to have produced all things, a foundation everlasting, self-existing, is consistent with reason, and I do not know that any better name than God . . . has yet been given.

The Human Situation
W. MACNEILE DIXON

If you believe in anything, you believe in God.

Author Unknown

If there is one Infinite . . . there cannot be another, for the other would limit the one, and thus render it finite, so as applied to God, the Eleatics argued: "If God is to be the mightiest and the best, he must be one, for if there were two or more, he would not be the mightiest and best." The Eleatics continued their monistic argument by showing that this One Infinite Being cannot be divided, so that anything could be called a portion of it, because there is no power that could separate anything from it. Nay, it cannot even have parts, for, as it has no beginning and no end, it can have no parts, for a part has a beginning and an end.

Max Müller, from Theosophy
Tertium Organum
P. D. OUSPENSKY

If we ask what is the highest purpose of the teachings of the Upanishads we can state it in three words, as it has been stated by the greatest Vedanta teachers themselves, namely "Tat twam asi." This means, Thou art That. "That" stands for that which is known to us under different names in different systems of ancient and modern philosophy. It is Zeus or the Eis Theos or To On in Greece; it is what Plato meant by the Eternal Idea, what Agnostics call the Unknowable, what I call the Infinite in Nature. This is what in India is called Brahman, the being behind all beings, the power that emits the universe, sustains it and draws it back again to itself. The Thou is what I call the Infinite in man, the Soul, the Self, the being behind every human Ego, free from all bodily fetters, free from passions, free from all attachments (Atman). The expression "Thou art That" means: thy soul is the Brahman; or in other words, the subject and the object of all being and of all knowing are one and the same.

Max Müller, from Theosophy
Tertium Organum
P. D. OUSPENSKY

Under and back of the universe of time and space and change, is ever to be found the Substantial Reality, the fundamental Truth. . . . Wise men call it the All.

The All must be all that Really is.

It is Infinite.

It is Immutable.

The All is in the earthworm, and yet the earthworm is far from being the All.

The Kabalion
HERMES TRISMEGISTUS

There is a thing inherent and natural,
Which existed before heaven and earth.
Motionless and fathomless,
It stands alone and never changes;

It pervades everywhere and never becomes exhausted.
It may be regarded as the Mother of the Universe.
I do not know its name.
If I am forced to give it a name,
I call it Tao, and I name it as supreme.

The Tao-Te King (Taoist scriptures)
Bible of the World

It is particularly interesting to note that the upanishadic authors claim that God did not say, "I shall create," but, rather, "I shall become," thus leaving their readers no option but to view all things as being somehow manifestations of the divine.

"I shall become many; I shall manifest myself in many forms."

Indian Philosophy and Modern Culture
PAUL BRUNTON

It is not I who live, but God lives in me.

ST. PAUL

The view of the Hindoos has been profounder than that of the Christians and Platonists. Their God is always creative and destructive at the same time. . . . If everyone feels that the constructive spirit is superior to the destructive, if most religions oppose the Devil to God, it is evidently because every life-unit, as long as it lasts, is on the whole constructive.

Problems of Personal Life
COUNT HERMANN KEYSERLING

If God were absolutely free there would be no creation. The Infinite Being has assumed unto Himself the mystery of finitude, and in him who is love, the finite and the infinite are one.

Sadhana
RABINDRANATH TAGORE

GOOD

Thou shalt serve God with the good impulse, and also with the evil impulse.

Jewish Wisdom

It is good for a man to open his mind to deep wonder and awe.

Rain Upon Godshill
J. B. Priestley
The New York Times Book Review, October 29, 1939

From the point of view of the good, pleasure and pain appear in a different meaning, so much so that pleasure may be shunned, and death itself made welcome, giving a higher value to life.

Sadhana
Rabindranath Tagore

Whatever is sown, whatever is cultivated, whatever is vitalized grows. This is true in the first instance of evil and its practice. But it is likewise true of the good. This must be cultivated without argument or fight with what opposes it.

Creative Understanding
Count Hermann Keyserling

GOVERNMENT

Socialism is necessary in order to broaden the basis for higher formation of problems. To stand fixed there belongs only to the nations which are still crude. In and for itself individualism stands as much above socialism as Christ's doctrine of the infinite value of the human soul does above the contemptuous attitude of antiquity toward the slave.

Europe
Count Hermann Keyserling

GREATNESS

The loftiest towers rise from the ground.

Chinese Proverb

Remember that a thing should always be itself; but it cannot be a big thing unless it suggests more than it really is. The secret of greatness lies in the power a thing has to suggest more than it says.

"The Most Unforgettable Character I've Met"
(Grandfather of Li Ying Ku, Secretary of Chiang Kai Shek)
MANUEL KOMROFF
Reader's Digest, April 1941

Everything great, and everything most worthwhile having, comes from a minority.

JOHANN WOLFGANG VON GOETHE

GRIEF

Shame, grief, bitterness, now revealed their mysterious mission; they had decomposed the earth, and they had fertilized it. The share of sorrow breaking the heart had opened up new sources of life. The waste land had once more burst into flowers. But they were not the old spring flowers. A new soul had been born.

Jean Christophe
ROMAIN ROLLAND

Grief comes to us all! And when it comes, there is but one way—to agree nobly with necessity.

The Splendour of Asia
L. ADAMS BECK

After giving way to the reasonable and natural impulses of your grief . . . adore His inscrutable, unfathomable, and all wise providence.

The Life of Mozart
EDWARD HOLMES

GROWTH

Touching the idea of natural growth of consciousness . . . (Dr. Bucke) does not notice that these faculties do not unfold themselves perforce: conscious work on them is necessary.

Tertium Organum
P. D. OUSPENSKY

The more the marble wastes,
The more the statue grows.

MICHELANGELO BUONARROTI

Christ was so against the Pharisees, because they were against growth.

Lecture
COUNT HERMANN KEYSERLING

Methinks I would not grow so fast,
Because sweet flowers are slow,
And weeds make haste.

King Richard III
WILLIAM SHAKESPEARE

HAPPINESS

The common denominator of human aspiration cannot be happiness attained (is it ever attained?), but only the way which leads to it, the kind of activity which renders us happy. Now this only possible and existing common denominator is creativeness.

Problems of Personal Life
COUNT HERMANN KEYSERLING

Where there is a capacity for enjoyment, there is a capacity for pain.

William Blake: His Philosophy and Symbols
S. Foster Damon

The highest enjoyment of man is not in the having but in the getting, which is at the same time not getting.

Sadhana
Rabindranath Tagore

It is only in marching on, that the man who has pluck can appease his ever unsatisfied heart with momentary joys.

Johann Wolfgang von Goethe

HEALTH

In my opinion there is only one reasonable and yet dignified attitude towards one's body and its accidents: That is to accept health and ill-health as equivalent facts and as alternatives equally devoid of value.

Problems of Personal Life
Count Hermann Keyserling

Only when endowed with an extremely strong physique has any great spirit ever been healthy.

America Set Free
Count Hermann Keyserling

Just to have health and happiness as objects in life, makes one no higher than the animals.

Lecture, Jan. 11, 1928
Count Hermann Keyserling

Humanity, kindness, brotherly sympathy are sometimes of more use to the patients than any medicine.

Fyodor Dostoevsky

HISTORY

Beethoven sings, Goethe observes, Chateaubriand is curious . . . and the world is changed. I suppose that the whole of history is due to . . . antagonism between exceptional thought which organizes, and ordinary action which does not.

Napoleon
Elie Faure

HOLY GHOST

We are no longer living in the age of the all-ruling Nature-Mother, the group; nor are we living any longer in that of the intermediary, the Son; we are living in the age of the Holy Ghost, when everyone must work out from within his own salvation, and the salvation of all.

Europe
Count Hermann Keyserling

HUMANITY

God keep us from judging. Humanity has not reached the age of reason and its efforts are still on the scale of the tribe.

Human Destiny
Lecomte du Noüy

HUMOR

He only has humor in the real sense, who knows how to give expression to a profound and even tragic opposition, from the vantage of a benevolent and serene mind. His is the quality of divine laughter of the man inwardly superior to those things ordinary people take with such fearsome seriousness. Accordingly there can be no high quality of humor unless intellectual understanding acts as the keynote.

America Set Free
Count Hermann Keyserling

IMAGINATION

What is imagination? Psychologists tell us that it is the plastic or creative power of the soul; but materialists confound it with fancy . . . which is the disorderly production of the material brain.

The Key to Theosophy, Feb. 1945
H. P. Blavatsky

God's prophets are poets . . . who have the courage to take their imaginings as truth.

William Blake: His Philosophy and Symbols
S. Foster Damon

Imagination is . . . an impartial workshop producing constructive or destructive manifestations, depending entirely on the will and direction of the one who owns it.

Today
Sara Robbins

Imagination makes us see, not with the eye, but through the eye.

William Blake

Man is the one animal endowed with free imagination.

Théophile Gautier

The world of imagination is the world of eternity.

William Blake

The stronger the imagination the less it is merely imaginary, and the more it is in harmony with truth.

Sadhana
Rabindranath Tagore

To know is nothing at all; to imagine everything.

ANATOLE FRANCE

Man consists of body, mind and imagination. His body is faulty, his mind untrustworthy, but his imagination has made him remarkable.

SOMERSET MAUGHAM

Imagination is more powerful than knowledge. Imagination enlarges your vision, stretches the mind, challenges the impossible. Without imagination, thought comes to a halt.

ALBERT EINSTEIN

Imagination gives to airy nothing a local habitation and a name.

WILLIAM SHAKESPEARE

INDIVIDUALITY

Gregariousness is always the refuge of mediocrity. Only individuals seek the truth.

Dr. Zhivago
BORIS PASTERNAK

INHERITANCE

We may dismiss the old debate as to whether environment is more important than heredity: Scientists now know that both have tremendous significance. They have discovered that living organisms inherit not actual characteristics so much as the tendency to produce the characteristics provided the environment is favorable.

"Heredity: The Hope of Mankind"
BRUCE BLIVEN
Reader's Digest, May, 1941

INSIGHT

Man in his fragile boat has the rudder placed in his hand just that he may not be at the mercy of the waves, but follow the direction of his own insight.

Life and Character
JOHANN WOLFGANG VON GOETHE

If a man wishes to attain to a higher insight, he must go beyond both the East and the West.

COUNT HERMANN KEYSERLING

INSPIRATION

When inspiration descends into the world of matter, it must be productive, or it is a great danger to the recipients.

William Blake: His Philosophy and Symbols
S. FOSTER DAMON

An artist should not wait for inspiration to paint, but must work continually: then when inspiration comes, he is ready.

KENNETH HAYES MILLER

INSTINCTS

Primeval instincts cannot change. (Among them proprietory instincts.) To protest against elementary nature is not a sign of profoundness, but merely of a lack of clear thinking.

Problems of Personal Life
COUNT HERMANN KEYSERLING

INTELLECT

The brain is that necessary prism, passing through which part of the psyche manifests itself to us as intellect. . . . The brain is a mirror, reflecting psychic life in our three-dimensional section of the world.

Tertium Organum
P. D. Ouspensky

Just as Shakespeare's greatest villains are pure intellects, so Blake's cosmic criminals are dominant Reason. Blake did not believe for a moment that Reason was intentionally or essentially bad, which is the position taken by so many mystics. . . . It is the domination of Reason; its usurpation of the throne which belongs to the spirit . . . its judging of all things by one standard—which makes it a bad thing.

William Blake: His Philosophy and Symbols
S. Foster Damon

We have every reason to believe that the men of the Cro-Magnon race who dominated northern Spain, France, and England between twenty-five and forty thousand years ago could compete in the art schools with any of the animal sculptors and painters of our day, and judging from the size and form of the brain of the Cro-Magnon youth I believe that they could enter any branch of the intellectual life of today on equal, if not superior, terms.

The Earth Speaks to Bryan
Henry Fairfield Osborn

We are now entering upon a new era. In the psychic organism of all men, the center of gravity has been shifted from the emotional to the intellectual.

The World in the Making
Count Hermann Keyserling

INTELLIGENCE

One-sided development of the intelligence has caused the entire soul-organism of western humanity to disintegrate. . . . Only one thing can help now, the deepening of our insight into things to such a degree that it will no longer work destructively, but constructively.

Europe
Count Hermann Keyserling

INTUITION

Intuition is not a sense in itself. It is simply the result of a rapid and accurate finding, produced through a fortunate combination of sense, impressions, and mental processes, telepathy included.

What's on Your Mind?
Joseph Dunninger

Intuition is the voice of the soul.

Intuition
Walter Newell Weston

The seat of the intuitive consciousness is not in the brain but in the solar plexis.

Intuition
Walter Newell Weston

Religion and art are . . . names for one and the same experience—an intuition of reality and of identity.

The Dance of Siva
Ananda Coomaraswamy

Intuition—the one faculty which establishes an immediate contact with the wholeness of life.

America Set Free
Count Hermann Keyserling

One can never know beforehand whether an insight intuitively gained is true or false. Later experience alone can prove its worth.

America Set Free
COUNT HERMANN KEYSERLING

Intuition leaves others as free as the freedom it exercises for itself.

Intuition
WALTER NEWELL WESTON

INVENTION

In invention every man "stands on the shoulders of other men."

Thomas A. Edison:
A Modern Olympian
MARY CHILDS NERNEY

ISOLATION

There is no such thing as absolute isolation in existence.

Sadhana
RABINDRANATH TAGORE

The least particle of truth colors the whole life. It is never isolated.

Sadhana
RABINDRANATH TAGORE

None of us liveth to himself, and no man dieth to himself.

PAUL
Romans 14:7

KNOWLEDGE

Knowledge has three degrees, opinion, science, illumination. The means or instrument of the first is sense; of the second dialectic; of the third intuition. To the last I subordinate reason. It is absolute knowledge founded on the identity of the mind knowing with the object known.

Tertium Organum
P. D. OUSPENSKY

Duality is the condition of our knowledge of the phenomenal world or the world of many dimensions.

Tertium Organum
P. D. OUSPENSKY

India has preserved a truth which we have forgotten, or denied. Knowledge and power may pass from man to man without speech.

Lancer at Large
FRANCIS YEATS-BROWN

Without going out of doors one may know the whole world.

Chinese Proverb

It is only when the cold season comes that we know the pine and cypress to be evergreens.

Chinese Proverb

The history of knowledge is a great fugue in which the voices of the nations, one after the other, emerge.

Life and Character
JOHANN WOLFGANG VON GOETHE

Little knowledge imparts to people pride; great knowledge imparts humility. Thus, ears empty of grain disdainfully lift up their heads to heaven, whereas those full bend theirs low, toward the earth their mother.

The Romance of Leonardo da Vinci
DMITRI MEREJKOWSKI

Science, philosophy, religion and art are forms of knowledge. The method of science is experiment; the method of philosophy is speculation; the method of religion and art is moral or esthetic emotional inspiration. But . . . [all] begin to serve true knowledge only when in them commence to manifest the sensing and finding of some inner property in things. In general it is quite possible to say—and perhaps it will be most true to fact—that the aim of every purely intellectual system of philosophy and science consists not at all in the giving to man of certain data of knowledge, but in the raising of man to such a height of thinking and feeling as to enable him to pass to those new and higher forms of knowledge to which art and religion approach more nearly. It is necessary, however, to remember that these very divisions into science, philosophy, religion and art betray the poverty and incompleteness of each.

Tertium Organum
P. D. OUSPENSKY

LANGUAGE

The formation of perceptions led to the formation of words, and the appearance of speech.

Tertium Organum
P. D. OUSPENSKY

The primitive races of mankind first employed the sign language, and spoken words; after that came picture language, and lastly the language of written words.

Minds and Manners of Wild Animals
WILLIAM TEMPLE HORNADAY

There can be no "monistic materialism." Materialism can be only dualistic, i.e., it must recognize two principles: motion and thought . . .

Our concepts are limited by language. Our language is deeply dualistic. . . . In our language only an eternally becoming universe exists. The "Eternal Now" cannot be expressed in language.

Tertium Organum
P. D. OUSPENSKY

LAW

Laws are only the rules of the game.

Lecture
COUNT HERMANN KEYSERLING

The beauty of a poem is bound by strict laws, yet it transcends them. The laws are its wings: they do not keep it weighed down; they carry it to freedom. Its form is in the law, but its spirit is in beauty.

Sadhana
RABINDRANATH TAGORE

The truly wise, knowing the nature of the universe, use Law against Law, the higher against the lower; and by the art of alchemy transmute that which is undesirable into that which is worthy, and thus triumph. Mastery consists not in abnormal dreams, visions, and fantastic imaginings, or living, but in using the higher forces against the lower, escaping the pains of the lower planes, by vibrating on the higher. Transmutation, not presumptuous denial, is the weapon of the master.

The Kabalion
HERMES TRISMEGISTUS

Higher laws transcend lower laws; i.e., they submerge or render them powerless.

Intuition
WALTER NEWELL WESTON

Everything happens according to law; chance is but a name for law not recognized; there are many planes of causation, but nothing escapes the law.

The Kabalion
HERMES TRISMEGISTUS

In all the universe there is no possibility of the breaking of natural law, but only of understanding and using its supernormal possibilities.

The House of Fulfilment
L. ADAMS BECK

The word supernatural implies the breaking or suspension of a law, and that can never be. The people of India would say they were supernormal—much above the common naturally, but strictly in conformity with a higher knowledge.

The Story of Oriental Philosophy
L. ADAMS BECK

God knows what fearful evils Adam and Eve may not have committed before they ate from the Tree of Knowledge; in any case it was not written down against them. Let every philosopher and every moralist ponder these facts. They seem to prove, and I think conclusively, that everything is permitted to a man, as long as he acts in accordance to the laws of his being, and as long as he acts in all innocence.

Europe
COUNT HERMANN KEYSERLING

LIBERTY

Liberty has been the criterion of evolution ever since the appearance of the original cell. It is toward liberty that the development of the personality of man tends toward an ever increasing independence. It is at the same time a goal and a tool. A goal because man must one day liberate himself from the despotism of the body. A tool because unless he is free to choose between good and evil, man cannot cooperate toward his own evolution, cannot improve himself deeply, from within.

Human Destiny
LECOMTE DU NOÜY

Where the Spirit of the Lord is, there is liberty.

PAUL
II Corinthians 3:17

It is from . . . mastery, based on the liberty to choose between the satisfaction of the appetites and the flight toward spirituality, that human dignity is born.

Human Destiny
LECOMTE DU NOÜY

LIFE

The beginning of thought . . . is that man does not simply accept his existence as something given, but experiences it as something unfathomably mysterious. Affirmation of life is the spiritual act by which man ceases to live unreflectively and begins to devote himself to his life with reverence in order to raise it to its true value.

Out of My Life and Thought
ALBERT SCHWEITZER

The man who has become a thinking being feels a compulsion to give to every will-to-live the same reverence for life, to promote life, to raise to its highest value life *which is capable of development;* and as being evil: to destroy life, to injure life, which is capable of development. This is the absolute fundamental principle of the moral, and it is a necessity of thought. . . . The world however offers us the horrible drama of Will-to-Live divided against itself. One existence holds its own at the cost of another. . . . But as an ethical being he strives to escape whenever possible . . . and as one who has become enlightened and merciful, to put a stop to this disunion.

Out of My Life and Thought
ALBERT SCHWEITZER

Life is a thought in the imagination of God.

The Vedantists

The meaning of life is in eternal search.

Tertium Organum
P. D. OUSPENSKY

The aim of life is life itself.

JOHANN WOLFGANG VON GOETHE

If you want a rich, full life you've got to gamble sometimes.

Born in Paradise
ARMINE VON TEMPSKI

Life's a grand adventure even when it goes against you.

Born in Paradise
ARMINE VON TEMPSKI

Minerals have life.

The Kabalion
HERMES TRISMEGISTUS

The choice, as Nietzsche saw so clearly, lies between a "yea-saying and a nay-saying to life." Men of sense will, I am persuaded, continue to accept rather than refuse.

The Human Situation
W. MACNEILE DIXON

In some sense every tendency leads to good; the perception of this significance in details is the fundamental problem of the art of life.

The Travel Diary of a Philosopher
COUNT HERMANN KEYSERLING

A "well-integrated" life does not mean a placid life, with all conflicts resolved. Many great souls have been inwardly tortured.

On Being a Real Person
HARRY EMERSON FOSDICK

Life always gets harder toward the summit—the cold increases, responsibility increases.

FRIEDRICH WILHELM NIETZSCHE

To live all one's life, to love all one's love, to die all one's death.

SAINT THERESA

Life seems so vulgar, so easily content with the commonplace things of everyday, and yet it always nurses and cherishes certain higher claims in secret, and looks about for the means of satisfying them.

Life and Character
JOHANN WOLFGANG VON GOETHE

We ought to live as straightforwardly as possible, as pluckily, as single-mindedly from within, as unconcerned for everything remote and external, as we can; the more we do this, the stronger and purer do we become. The less a man relies upon alien forces, the more he takes upon his own shoulders, the more does nature smile upon him.

The Travel Diary of a Philosopher
COUNT HERMANN KEYSERLING

If we consider life as one whole, certainly Self-realization must be regarded as its essential purpose from the beginning.

The Dance of Siva
ANANDA COOMARASWAMY

In obeying the will-to-live we are fulfilling divine orders.

The Human Situation
W. MACNEILE DIXON

Life should be considered an art; and we should create the circumstances, with which to overcome difficulties.

JOHN DEWEY
"Invitation to Learning" radio program, Oct. 12, 1958

LIGHT

Illumination is more than a state of emotion; it is a state of knowledge as well.

William Blake: His Philosophy and Symbols
S. FOSTER DAMON

The light which puts out our eyes is darkness to us. There is more day to dawn. The sun is but a morning star.

Walden
HENRY DAVID THOREAU

LIMITS

Man has found out the great paradox that what is limited is not imprisoned within its limits; it is ever moving and therewith shedding its finitude every moment.

Sadhana
RABINDRANATH TAGORE

The most insignificant man can be complete if he works within the limits of his capacities. . . . But even fine talents can be obscured and neutralized, and destroyed by lack of this indispensable requirement of symmetry.

Life and Character
JOHANN WOLFGANG VON GOETHE

LIVING

If you take on the job of living one day at a time, you'll make it.

"I Always Have Help,"
Anonymous Article
Saturday Evening Post, May 21, 1960

LOAFING

I loaf and invite my soul.

WALT WHITMAN

From dawn to dusk I sit here before my door, and I know that of a sudden the happy moment will arrive, when I shall see.

Gitanjali
RABINDRANATH TAGORE

LOGIC

Logic, or the science of concepts, is that system which studies the qualitative (categorical) relations between things.

Tertium Organum
P. D. OUSPENSKY

Concept: An abstract general notion or idea; also, any notion combining elements into the idea of one object.

Funk and Wagnalls Practical Standard Dictionary

Without experience, logic wanders in the void.

The Human Situation
W. MACNEILE DIXON

The recognition of the reality of . . . divisions is necessary for the acceptance of the fundamental axioms of the logic of Aristotle and Bacon, i.e., the absolute and incontestable recognition of the duality of the world—of dualism.

The recognition of the unreality of these divisions and that of the unity of all opposites is necessary for the comprehension of higher logic.

Tertium Organum
P. D. OUSPENSKY

LOVE

Love is understanding.

America Set Free
Count Hermann Keyserling

Set me as a seal upon thine heart, as a seal upon thine arm: for love is strong as death . . . . Many waters cannot quench love, neither can the floods drown it: if a man would give all the substance of his house for love, it would utterly be contemned.

The Song of Solomon 8:6-7

The Indians have declared that the path of love is easiest for man . . . The path of recognition is considered the higher, and love does not count nearly as much as it does among us.

Count Hermann Keyserling

I do not love him because he is good, but because he is my little child.

The Crescent Moon
Rabindranath Tagore

Let your love see me,
Even through the barrier
Of nearness.

Rabindranath Tagore

We may say that a merely negligible part of love's energy goes into posterity; the greater part is spent by the fathers and mothers on their personal emotions as it were. . . .

Moreover—and this perhaps is the most important—the superfluous energy is not wasted at all, but is transformed into other forms of energy, possible to discover. Generally speaking, the significance of the indirect results may very often be of more importance than the significance of the direct ones. And since we are able to trace how the energy of love transforms itself into instincts, ideas, creative forces on different planes of life; into symbols of art, song, music, poetry; so can we easily imagine how the same energy may transform itself into a higher order of intuition, into a higher consciousness which will reveal to us a marvelous and mysterious world.

Tertium Organum
P. D. OUSPENSKY

The great emotion in Eternity is that of Brotherhood. To love is impossible on the highest plane because it necessitates a separation of lover and beloved, which is a descent. . . . However love on this earth is a reuniting, and of course an ascent.

William Blake: His Philosophy and Symbols
S. FOSTER DAMON

MAN

Man ultimately is nothing but spirit.

America Set Free
COUNT HERMANN KEYSERLING

Man needs to be privileged to live normally.

Problems of Personal Life
COUNT HERMANN KEYSERLING

Man is the one animal capable of error.

THÉOPHILE GAUTIER

If we were to interpret the so-called Fall of Man as a fortunate rather than a lamentable occurrence, if we were to call it rather his coming of age, the moment at which he took upon himself his natural duties and responsibilities, matters might begin to wear a sensibly brighter appearance.

The Human Situation
W. MACNEILE DIXON

During a prolonged study of the lives of various men both great and small, I came upon this thought: In the web of the world the one may well be regarded as the warp, the other as the woof. It is the little man, after all, who gives breadth to the web, and the great men firmness and solidity; perhaps also the addition of some sort of pattern. But the scissors of the fates determine the length, and to that all . . . must join in submitting itself.

Life and Character
JOHANN WOLFGANG VON GOETHE

The ideal humanity will never be a melting pot, but an harmonious orchestration.

RABBI GOLDSTEIN

I should suit [the mass] better if I suited myself less. I feel that the public demands an average man, average thoughts and manners—not originality, nor even absolute excellence. You cannot interest them except as you are like them, and sympathize with them.

Thoreau's Journal, Dec. 6, 1854
HENRY DAVID THOREAU

Certain faults are necessary to the individual if he is to exist.

Life and Character
JOHANN WOLFGANG VON GOETHE

The strong man is he who can intercept at will the communications between his senses and his thoughts.

Napoleon
ELIE FAURE

At all times it has not been the age, but the individuals alone who have worked for knowledge. It was the age which put Socrates to death by poison, the age which burnt Huss. The ages have always remained alike.

Life and Character
JOHANN WOLFGANG VON GOETHE

A man must be as objective toward his own nature as a chemist is toward the chemicals, whose properties he studies. And like him one should see in one's personal qualities, the elements which can be combined into a new and higher synthesis.

The World in the Making
COUNT HERMANN KEYSERLING

Compared with what we ought to be, we are only half awake. We are making use of only a small part of our physical and mental resources. Stating the thing broadly, the human individual thus lives far within his limits. He possesses powers of various sorts which he habitually fails to use.

The Varieties of Religious Experience
WILLIAM JAMES

No well integrated life is possible . . . without an initial act of self acceptance, as though to say: I, John Smith, hereby accept myself, with my inherited endowments and handicaps . . . and so accepting myself, as my stint, I will now see what I can do with this John Smith.

On Being a Real Person
HARRY EMERSON FOSDICK

The special significance of the individual wherever it [is specially significant] consists in this, that owing to his special adjustment and aptitude, he is better able than others to recognize and express, in thought and act, definite, generally significant possibilities of development, so to this extent it plays the role of an organ of the collective whole.

The World in the Making
COUNT HERMANN KEYSERLING

The enormous majority of the population of this globe is engaged in effect in destroying, disfiguring, and falsifying the ideas of the minority. The majority is without ideas. It is incapable of understanding the ideas of the minority, and left to itself it must inevitably disfigure and destroy. . . . Creation and destruction—or more correctly, the ability to create or the ability only to destroy—are the principal signs of the two types of men.

Tertium Organum
P. D. OUSPENSKY

Our attachment to sensual pleasures which recall our origin afford the proof that we are still at the beginning of human evolution. The fact that certain individuals have revolted against this physiological slavery demonstrates that something else exists within us.

Human Destiny
LECOMTE DU NOÜY

Whoso would be a man must be a non-conformist.

RALPH WALDO EMERSON

A gathering of a hundred highly intelligent men, taken together, make one single idiot. Because every gift, whether intellectual or moral, is in the first instance a question of individual differentiation.

DR. JONG

Every individual is fundamentally unique. Accordingly if he identifies himself with what is common to all, he voluntarily renounces his intrinsic value, and this inevitably leads to a lowering of his level.

America Set Free
COUNT HERMANN KEYSERLING

Difficulty attracts the man of character because it is in embracing it that he realizes himself.

The Florida Times Union, Jan. 29, 1961
CHARLES DE GAULLE

The man with strong passions lives them, while the man with weak passions is lived by them.

In the Introduction to
Miguel de Unamuno's
"The Tragic Sense of Life"
SALVADOR DE MADARIAGA

People are not ruled by their institutions but by their characters.

GUSTAVE LE BON

A man can be a general favorite only in two cases: either if he is a saint or else if he is quite commonplace without any signs of superiority of any kind.

America Set Free
COUNT HERMANN KEYSERLING

The individual at every moment of his being, actually reflects a cosmic situation.

The World in the Making
COUNT HERMANN KEYSERLING

Man is spirit in his innermost depths; he is a being of gana, sensitive, emotional, intellectual; all these strata and all these parts are equally his; only they are so on different planes, and a man lives on all these planes at the same time. . . . The integral revelation for which man is ripe today . . . is that which reveals the true and just relations between the diverse layers of his total being.

Problems of Personal Life
COUNT HERMANN KEYSERLING

We feel . . . despair only when we begin to regard man as something "finite," finished; when we see nothing beyond man, and think that we know everything about him. In such form the problem is truly a desperate one.

Tertium Organum
P. D. OUSPENSKY

Henceforth contrary to all the others [animals] in order to evolve he [man] must no longer obey Nature. He must criticize and control his desires which were previously the only Law.

Human Destiny
LECOMTE DU NOÜY

To this extent does everything depend on man's attitude toward himself; that which he will not affirm within himself can never develop.

The World in the Making
COUNT HERMANN KEYSERLING

The only goal of man should be the attainment of human dignity with all its implications.

Human Destiny
LECOMTE DU NOÜY

To live as one likes is plebeian; the noble man aspires to order and law.

JOHANN WOLFGANG VON GOETHE

The inferior man regulates his life by externals. . . . The superior man is of another sort, and of him it may be said, with Chuang Tzu, "that they live in accordance with their own nature. In the whole world they have no equal. They regulate their life by inward things."

The Dance of Siva
ANANDA COOMARASWAMY

I think everyone should do the best they can and trust to the Superior Intelligence that rules the Universe to attend to the hereafter.

Thomas A. Edison:
A Modern Olympian
MARY CHILDS NERNEY, *quoting*
Thomas A. Edison

Every original worker in intellectual fields, every man who makes some new thing, is certain to arouse hostility where he does not meet with indifference.

Thomas A. Edison:
A Modern Olympian
MARY CHILDS NERNEY, *quoting*
Thomas A. Edison

[An] idea which has now been refuted by events [is] that good institutions form accomplished men of their own accord.

Problems of Personal Life
COUNT HERMANN KEYSERLING

MATHEMATICS

The problem of mathematics is the problem of world order.

In the Introduction to
P. D. Ouspensky's
"Tertium Organum"
CLAUDE BRAGDON

MATTER

Matter, or substance, is now defined as energy at a certain velocity.

The Human Situation
W. MACNEILE DIXON

What is matter? From one point of view, it is a logical concept, i.e., a form of thinking. Nobody ever saw matter, nor will they ever—it is possible only to think matter. From another point of view it is an illusion accepted for reality. Even more truly, it is the incorrectly perceived form of that which exists in reality. Matter is a section of something; a nonexistent, imaginary section. But that of which matter is a section, exists. This is the real, four-dimensional world.

Tertium Organum
P. D. OUSPENSKY

The atom was blasted in 1919 by Rutherford when he literally knocked H out of nitrogen. The H in this case stands for hydrogen.

This was the first artificial transmutation of matter.

The Advance of Science
Formerly edited by WATSON DAVIS, *Director of Science Service, Washington, D.C.*

MATURITY

When the melon is ripe it will drop of itself.

Chinese Proverb

The greed for the fruit misses the flower.

RABINDRANATH TAGORE

MEANING

We must know that it is only the revelation of the Infinite which is endlessly new, and eternally beautiful, in us, which gives the only meaning to ourselves.

Sadhana
RABINDRANATH TAGORE

All knowledge is relative. We can never grasp all the meanings of any one thing, because in order to grasp them all, it is necessary for us to grasp the whole world, with all the variety of meanings contained in it. . . .

Tertium Organum
P. D. OUSPENSKY

[The] realization of intrinsic meaning, as deep as possible but ever personal, is the only aim of all individual life.

Problems of Personal Life
COUNT HERMANN KEYSERLING

MEASUREMENT

"Large" and "small," what is the meaning of these words? None save the meaning we give them. And what is the unit of these measurements? the unit we assign.

The Human Situation
W. MACNEILE DIXON

MEMORY

Memory has never been located as a power within the brain. No examination of the body or brain in health or disease, yields any information on this faculty of recollection; no physical theory accounts for it. I look for a moment at a ship upon the sea, and then turn away. I can still, however, if I wish, see it in the mind's eye.

The Human Situation
W. MACNEILE DIXON

Mere information . . . gets disposed of by every process of genuine understanding. It is digested, transformed into organic form, and the greater the perfection of the process, the more will the conscious of today descend to the unconscious regions—hence the so-called deficient memory, the constant complaint of all creative minds.

The Recovery of Truth
COUNT HERMANN KEYSERLING

The man into whom we seek to infuse a living impulse should not have so much explained to him, that he can store the meaning of what has been said into his memory—for there it loses its transforming power.

The World in the Making
COUNT HERMANN KEYSERLING

Elephants never forget.

MRS. POWERS,
a former elephant trainer speaking on the Bessie Beatty Radio Broadcast, 1941

To me it is ridiculous to exalt memory so that in time a parrot may well be held the wisest of the Lord's creatures.

CHARLES E. BOEHM, *Penn. Super. of Public Instruction*
Saturday Evening Post, May 14, 1960

METAPHYSICS

Metaphysics is the study of the ultimate reality of all things.

The Story of Philosophy
WILL DURANT

The metaphysical reality is essentially and purely inward, to be understood from within only. The West has never quite clearly been aware of this.

COUNT HERMANN KEYSERLING

There is an intimate connection between the depth of thought and that of tone. Just as one profound thought controls from within a thousand superficial ones, so an infinite number of melodies can be conceived in higher keys of one single basic tone, whereas every given melody in the treble is related to only one in the base. Modern music is entirely confined to the treble, and only lets one imagine basic tones indirectly: that of Bach is nothing but a single basic tone, and to this extent it is the foundation of all other music. No musician has ever been as deep as Bach; to the metaphysician he is therefore more congenial than any other. For the metaphysician has to play the base in the symphony of the spirit of recognition, to find and sound the basic tones in the music of the world.

The Travel Diary of a Philosopher
COUNT HERMANN KEYSERLING

MIND

The universe is mental.

The Kabalion
HERMES TRISMEGISTUS

Mind is senior to the world, and the architect thereof.

RALPH CUDWORTH

All life is mind, all development differing degrees of concentration.

The House of Fulfilment
L. Adams Beck

It is no longer forbidden us to think of nature as a grand society, a hierarchy, and to say that everywhere mind acts not upon dead matter but at all times directly upon mind.

The Human Situation
W. Macneile Dixon

It is the mind that makes us wise or ignorant, bound or emancipated. One is holy because of his mind, one is a sinner because of his mind.

The Works of Sri Ramakrishna
(Hindu Scriptures)
The Bible of the World

The mind itself has a higher state of existence beyond reason, a superconscious state and . . . when the mind gets to the higher state, then this knowledge beyond reason comes. . . . All the different steps to Yoga are intended to bring us scientifically to the superconscious state of Samadhi. . . . Just as unconscious work is beneath consciousness, so there is another work which is above consciousness, and which also is not accompanied with the feeling of egoism.

The Varieties of Religious Experience
William James

MISFORTUNE

A gem is not polished without rubbing, nor a man perfected without trials.

Chinese Proverb

Events are never absolute—their results depend entirely on the individual: Misfortune is a stepping stone to the genius; a cleansing to the Christian; a treasure to the shrewd man; an abyss to the weak.

César Birotteau
Honoré de Balzac

Bose takes a mimosa, shields it from harmful contacts, allows it to grow up in ideal conditions. Apparently it is a prosperous plant, but appearances are deceptive. It lacks the bracing buffets of wind, the sudden changes of temperature, the variety of an unsheltered life: there is a slowing-down of its vital force, its nervous reflex arc has contracted, there is a weakness in its fibre. In short, it has degenerated, just as a man or a woman does whose character has not been tempered in the fire of adversity.

Lancer at Large
Francis Yeats-Brown

MORALITY

Morality should be the co-ordination and the necessity for co-ordination of all sides of life.

Tertium Organum
P. D. Ouspensky

Morality, the aim of which is to establish a system of correct relations toward the emotions, and to assist in their purification and elevation, ceases in our eyes to be some wearisome and self-limiting exercise in virtue. Morality—this is a form of esthetics.

That which is not moral is first of all not beautiful, because not concordant, not harmonious.

Tertium Organum
P. D. Ouspensky

In reading a work on agriculture, I skip the author's moral reflections, and the words "Providence" and "He" scattered along the page, to come to the profitable level of what he has to say. There is no science in men's religion; it does not teach us so much as the report of the committee on swine. My author shows he has dealt in corn and turnips, and worshipped God with the hoe and spade, but spare me his morality.

Thoreau's Journal, April 1, 1841
HENRY DAVID THOREAU

Morality is that which strengthens. Immorality is that which weakens.

COMPLETE WORKS OF
SWAMI VIVEKANANDA

A great man, being different in kind from the ordinary person, the moral law expressive of his true connection with the world must also be different. What is generally called "morality" is really only middle-class morality. The middle-class type of man must have rigid rules of conduct; first, because he is not sufficiently differentiated to centralize and direct his nature from within; second, because he cannot rise to a superior kind of form and ardor. The reason why great men so often seem immoral is that all creative geniuses are of necessity artist natures. This implies not only advantages but idiosyncracies as well. The spirit principle, being opposed to the law of matter, will not endure executive routine; and most systems of morals presuppose a life of routine and executive actions as a matter of course. Then they must be extreme individualists, and there is no common denominator for individual esthetics and social morality. Above all they are in need of stimulation. . . . This, then, leads to the profoundest cause of the artist's so-called immorality. The artist really lives for his work in the same sense that the pregnant woman lives for her child. Accordingly, that only is the right thing for him to do or to submit to which helps the child to grow. Now the birth of a poem is far from being valuable to the man in the street.

America Set Free
Count Hermann Keyserling

MULTIPLICITY

There are millions of stars so immense that room could be found for millions of our petty suns in one of them.

The Human Situation
W. Macneile Dixon

The physicists and psychologists emulate the astronomers and paralyze our faculties with a like arithmetic. There is an inner deep to match the outer. A drop of water confounds us. It contains millions upon millions of molecules, and you may say galaxies of electrons. Each live cell in our bodies is composed of three hundred billion atoms.

The Human Situation
W. Macneile Dixon

MUSIC

Music is the language of the soul.

Romain Rolland

The emotional tones of life, i.e., of "feelings," are best transmitted by music, but it cannot express concepts, i.e., thought.

Tertium Organum
P. D. Ouspensky

Music—that victorious recovery of man's talent for organization over the chaos of his passions.

Napoleon
ELIE FAURE

Music is a higher revelation than all wisdom and philosophy. . . . The one incorporeal entrance into the higher world which comprehends mankind, but which mankind cannot comprehend.

LUDWIG VAN BEETHOVEN

The master musicians of India are always represented as the pupils of a god, or as visiting the heaven world to learn there the music of the spheres—that is to say, their knowledge springs from a source far within the surface of the empirical activity of the waking consciousness.

The Dance of Siva
ANANDA COOMARASWAMY

Passionate music of the nightingale,
Not joy you bring me, but a strange regret,
A memory of nothingness,
The pale face of a lover I have never met.

From the Japanese

NATURE

Throughout nature all events are separate events, and between them no logical or necessary nexus can be discovered. The link or bond is established in our minds, by our expectations, by our previous observations, of such a conjunction.

The Human Situation
W. MACNEILE DIXON

The essence of modern science, Sir James Jeans tells us, is that man no longer sees nature as something distinct from himself.

The Human Situation
W. MACNEILE DIXON

Like wind and sunsets, wild things were taken for granted until progress began to do away with them. Now we face the question whether a still higher standard of living is worth its cost in things natural, wild and free. For us of the minority, the opportunity to see geese is more important than television, and the chance to find a pasque flower a right as inalienable as free speech.

"A Sand County Almanac"
ALDO LEOPOLD
Reader's Digest, March 1961

Only the ignorant and the blind believe that the soil ever comes to rest. . . . That life force also pulsates in us, an intensely profound and irresistible force. We belong to her and she belongs to us. . . . It is through her that mounts in us the spirit of our forebears. Half our misery derives from the fact that we have broken with the soil.

That Day Alone
PIERRE VAN PAASSEN

Viewed merely in an external and experimental fashion, the high civilization of antiquity had ended in the learning of a certain lesson; that is, in its conversion to Christianity. But that lesson was a psychological fact as well as a theological fact. That pagan civilization had indeed been a very high civilization. It would not weaken our thesis, it might even strengthen it, to say it was the highest humanity ever reached. It had discovered its still unrivaled arts of poetry and plastic representation; it had discovered its own political ideals; it had discovered its own clear system of logic and of language. But above all, it had discovered its own mistake.

That mistake was too deep to be ideally defined; the shorthand of it is to call it the mistake of nature-worship. It might almost as truly be called the mistake of being natural.

St. Francis of Assisi
GILBERT K. CHESTERTON

There can be nothing dead or mechanical in nature. If in general life and feeling exist, they must exist in all. Life and rationality make up the world.

Tertium Organum
P. D. OUSPENSKY

Nature has, like ourselves, her days and nights, and months and years, her seasons of rising sap and flowery spring, of autumnal withdrawals and slumber before another dawn. . . . We have not found the measure of nature's cycles, and fix no dates for her recurrences. They are too vast for our scale. Death will overtake her, say our modern instructors, and doubtless they are right. But her death will be a sleep. Refreshed, she will shake her hyacinthine locks, and rising, get to her task again.

The Human Situation
W. MACNEILE DIXON

Heraclitus taught, as we have seen, that men were wrong who praised and sought the easy path, the putting off of burdens, escape from effort and anxiety, from hardships. . . . They were wrong since, though they knew it not, they asked for the end of the world. And to their foolishness they added a pusillanimous desire for idleness, for wages they had not earned, a check for everlasting enjoyment. Men cry out for a felicity they have done nothing to deserve, a felicity moreover under lock and key safe forever. But whatever it may have been, it was manifestly not nature's design to establish a pauper colony of idlers on the dole. She provided, in the phrase of Keats, "a vale of soul-making."

The Human Situation
W. MACNEILE DIXON

Modern man should somehow make his peace with the earth on which he lives. Modern civilization more than any which has gone before lives visibly and dangerously beyond its means. This does not signify merely that we are using up natural resources. It means that we are disturbing a delicate balance of things, a harmony which has got itself established by trial and error, and which has not previously been subjected to the cataclysmic activities of creatures literally able to move mountains. Man can undo in a year or so what nature has taken hundreds, even thousands, of years to bring about. There is an interdependence of living things. We can't go on if we upset the balance of nature too much.

R. L. DUFFUS
N. Y. Times Book Review, Dec. 12, 1937

Henceforth, in order to evolve man must no longer obey Nature. He must criticize and control his desires which were previously the only law.

Human Destiny
LECOMTE DU NOÜY

If man cannot definitely transform the age in which he has conquered nature into one rung higher on the ladder that leads him up to the spiritual world, then that which appears to be progress will mean a fall.

America Set Free
COUNT HERMANN KEYSERLING

Nature always possesses a certain sonorousness as in the hum of insects, the booming of ice, the crowing of cocks in the morning, and the barking of dogs in the night, which indicates her sound state. God's voice is but a clear bell sound. The effect of the slightest tinkling in the horizon measures my own soundness. I thank God for sound; it always mounts, and makes me mount. I think I will not trouble myself for any wealth when I can be so cheaply enriched.

Thoreau's Journal, March 3, 1841
HENRY DAVID THOREAU

Whether we think of ourselves and our private lives, or of mankind in general, we perceive how closely human destiny is associated with the pulsing energies of nature, of which we are for the most part unconscious. . . . From the depths of space, from the farthest star, influences pour down upon us, as in cosmic radiation, from sources at which we can but dimly guess. How significant is the cycle of sunspots, some so large that all the planets might find room in one of them. Do they attract even our idle wonder? Yet they, like all things, have their pulse, and are more numerous, Sir James Jeans tells us, at intervals of about eleven years, as they were in 1928 and will be again in 1939. You suppose them to be unimportant. Yet they hold the fates of all men in the hollow of their mighty hands. Our terrestrial weather follows their surging rhythm and—as has been proved by the ring growths of ancient trees—change from cold to wet, to warmth to dry, in response to this periodic activity.

The Human Situation
W. MACNEILE DIXON

NECESSITY

If it were not for the compulsion of personal necessity very few men, if any, would ever have given up the whole of their lives to the mission for all.

COUNT HERMANN KEYSERLING

In order that a house and grounds may be picturesque and interesting in the highest degree, they must suggest the idea of necessity, proving the devotion of the builder, not of luxury. We need to see the honest and naked life here and there protruding. What is a fort without any foe before it, that is not now sustaining, and never has sustained a siege?

Thoreau's Journal, March 20, 1858
HENRY DAVID THOREAU

OBEDIENCE

He who best employs people, is obedient himself.

LAO-TZU

OCCULT

The more we discover of the hidden forces of nature, the more important does it become to understand; that it is spiritually quite irrelevant, not only whether we are clairvoyant or blind, but also whether there are gods or not. To-day, it is more important than ever to take to heart what Christ and Buddha have said against the workers of miracles; both have emphasized repeatedly that we are not concerned with psychic development, but with something else belonging with a different dimension. All squinting at the supernatural is derogatory. Only those free from bias can advance.

The Travel Diary of a Philosopher
COUNT HERMANN KEYSERLING

OPPOSITION

The principal of polarity. . . . Everything has its poles; everything has its pair of opposites; like and unlike are the same; extremes meet; all truths are but half truths; all paradoxes may be reconciled.

The mental state belongs to innumerable classes, each class of which has its opposite poles, along which transmutation is possible. Poles may be classified as positive and negative. Thus love is positive to hate.

The Kabalion
HERMES TRISMEGISTUS

The human mind requires contrary expressions against which to test itself.

One World
WENDELL L. WILLKIE

All energies had their contraries, and from the strain their opposition engendered the world had arisen. In a word, no opposition, no world. These rival forces were, in fact, the two inseparable halves of the same thing as are the concave and convex sides of a curve, they were contrary yet complementary activities, which by their union in disunion produce an attainment, a hidden harmony. . . . For that which strives against another in reality supports itself. As heat implies cold, justice implies injustice.

The Human Situation
W. MACNEILE DIXON

Nothing without opposition can become manifest to itself.

JAKOB BÖHME

"Two great talkers will not travel far together," is a Spanish saying; I will add, nor two silent people; we naturally love our opposites.

Lavengro
George Borrow

ORIGINALITY

True originality . . . rests on the vitalization of a phenomenon, be that phenomenon new or unknown from a new depth of meaning.

Europe
Count Hermann Keyserling

PERFECTION

There are two main paths leading to perfection. One through emotion, the other intellect.

Mrs. Frank Cobb
Radio Broadcast, Dec. 5, 1937

PHILOSOPHY

Philosophy is synthetic interpretation.

The Story of Philosophy
Will Durant

He had regarded thought as "a mere pensioner of outward form." Now into the broad sunlight emerged a menacing, incontrovertible truth that in the picture he drew of nature he was invariably himself present, and that his presence gave to the picture features which virgin nature never had, nor could have. In a word science discovered philosophy in which it had steadfastly refused to believe.

The Human Situation
W. Macneile Dixon

This time salvation will not come from any new faith however great the longing for it may be. The new synthesis of mind and soul must originate from the mind, on the height of supreme intellectuality, if something decisive is to happen. What follows is this: The important task today is not assigned to religion, but to philosophy.

Creative Understanding
COUNT HERMANN KEYSERLING

Philosophy means and includes five fields of study:

Logic—Ideal method of thought
Ethics—Ideal conduct
Politics—Ideal social organization
Esthetics—Ideal form of beauty
Metaphysics—Ultimate reality of all things

The Story of Philosophy
WILL DURANT

PLEASURES

There's night and day, brother, both sweet things; sun, moon, and stars, brother, all sweet things; there's likewise a wind on the heath. Life is very sweet, brother.

Lavengro
GEORGE BORROW

Do you remember the enchantment when you were a child, of waking one morning in a strange, muffled, bluish world, to find snow blanketing everything? The beginnings of journeys are delightful, settling down in a railroad carriage, or having a preliminary prowl over the ship. But better still is coming home after a long absence, the moment you open your own front door. Then there's the delicious moment in the theatre, when the orchestra is fiddling away at the overture, and the footlights have been turned up so that at the bottom of the curtain there's a magic brightness, suggesting the immediate possibility of every kind of enchantment.

"The Minor Pleasures of Life"
J. B. PRIESTLEY
Reader's Digest, Oct. 1, 1939

'Tis my faith that every flower enjoys the air it breathes.

WILLIAM WORDSWORTH

POETRY

Poets are the mirrors of the gigantic shadows which futurity casts upon the present.

PERCY BYSSHE SHELLEY

True prophets were simply poets who beheld the eternal truths by power of imagination.

WILLIAM BLAKE

Poetry endeavors to express both music and thought together.

Tertium Organum
P. D. OUSPENSKY

The escape from literalism is through the simile. The poet who uses this compares his object to some other object, and thus obtains some sort of connection [though a weak one] with the rest of the universe. Moreover, he can invoke all sorts of things as contributing effects to his main sensation.

Higher yet is the metaphor, which by eliminating the conjunctive words like *to* and *as* practically identifies the object with its emotional equivalent.

The symbol however uses the identity, yet discards the named object for the Eternity which is thus invoked. It is the highest degree in the poetic scale.

Practically the whole existence of poetry consists in this imposing of human values upon natural objects.

William Blake: His Philosophy and Symbols
S. Foster Damon

Poets work intuitively.

William Blake

Chinese poetry is of all poetry I know the most human and the least symbolic or romantic. It contemplates life just as it presents itself, without any veil of ideas, any rhetoric or sentiment; it simply clears away the obstruction which habit has built up between us and the beauty of things.

An Essay on the Civilization of India, China and Japan
Goldsworthy Lowes Dickinson

The poet must recognize that his state is neither more nor less than a waking sleep. And indeed I do not deny that a great many things have come to my knowledge when I was in a dream-like condition.

Johann Wolfgang von Goethe

Verse a breeze mid blossoms straying from youth and age.

Samuel Taylor Coleridge

Poets are fierce people. They are individualistic, and yet given to universal thinking; and their individualism after all is a mental affair. . . . They have the nervous energy and the imagination of the sensitive man.

Edgar Allan Poe

With me poetry has been not a purpose but a passion; and the passions should be held in reverence: they must not —they cannot at will be excited, with an eye to the paltry compensations, or the more paltry commendations of mankind.

Poems, 1831. Introduction
Letters to Mrs. B.
EDGAR ALLAN POE

The poet understands that the mast of a ship, the gallows, and the cross are made of different wood. He understands the difference between the stone from a church wall and a stone from a prison wall. He hears "the voice of stones," understands the whisperings of ancient walls, of tumuli, of mountains, rivers, woods and plains. He hears "the voice of the silence," understands the psychological difference between silences, knows that one silence can differ from another. And this poetical understanding of the world should be developed, strengthened and fortified, because only by its aid do we come in contact with the true world of reality. In the real world, behind phenomena which appear to us similar, often stand noumena so different that only by our blindness is it possible to account for our idea of the similarity of those phenomena.

Tertium Organum
P. D. OUSPENSKY

PRAYER

Prayer is communion with God.

Prayer
GEORGE A. BUTTERICK

A few minutes of conscious abstraction every morning, effects more than severest training through work. This explains among other things, the strengthening effects of prayer.

The Travel Diary of a Philosopher
COUNT HERMANN KEYSERLING

Be not forgetful of prayer. Every time you pray, if your prayer is sincere, there will be new feeling and new meaning in it, which will give you fresh courage, and you will understand that prayer is an education.

FYODOR DOSTOEVSKY

Old Hayden went down on his knees each morning before he took pen in hand. Watch and pray. Keep in pious and loving communion with the spirit of life.

ROMAIN ROLLAND

The normal life heightened was Blake's ideal. He never lost his grip on the world. Even his ecstasies came uninvoked. He left no system of meditation or magic ceremonies to evoke deity; prayer was his sole method.

William Blake: His Philosophy and Symbols
S. FOSTER DAMON

Let me love Thee alone, O Lord.

Prayer of All the Devotees

From people who merely pray we must become people who bless.

FRIEDRICH NIETZSCHE

Pray for serenity to accept things we can't change, and for courage to change things we can.

"I Always Have Help"
Anonymous article on A.A.
Saturday Evening Post, May 21, 1960

PRIORITY

First things first.

The Art of Practical Thinking
RICHARD WEIL

heights. . . . The world has found the mathematical approach and calls this the fourth dimension. . . . In a word, science is beginning to explain by the mathematical approach what the Buddha, the Christ, St. Paul, and others saw . . . the reality that lay beyond.

The House of Fulfilment
L. Adams Beck

The unyielding sureness of reality sometimes crosses our will, and very often leads us to disaster, just as the firmness of the earth invariably hurts the falling child who is learning to walk. Nevertheless, it is the same firmness that hurts him, that makes his walking possible.

Sadhana
Rabindranath Tagore

Not all reality but a simplified edition of its fundamental features is open to us, and the world of space and time thus resembles an artist's picture. There a part of the boundless and representable landscape of reality is reduced and separated from the whole and framed for our contemplation.

The Human Situation
W. Macneile Dixon

Exterior reality is just as real as interior.

Problems of Personal Life
Count Hermann Keyserling

Not all can learn to discern the real from the false; but he who can will not receive the gift of discernment free. This is a thing of great labor, a thing of great work, which demands boldness of thought and boldness of feeling.

Tertium Organum
P. D. Ouspensky

The new era rigidly demands the readjustment of the human depth to reality.

Europe
COUNT HERMANN KEYSERLING

RECOGNITION

Recognition does not lead to salvation, but is salvation.

The Travel Diary of a Philosopher
COUNT HERMANN KEYSERLING

REFORMERS

If reformers had a sense of humor, it is not likely they would be reformers.

The American Mind in Action, quoted in America Set Free
COUNT HERMANN KEYSERLING

REINCARNATION

Even the believer in reincarnation does not assert that the same person progresses from incarnation to incarnation (no matter how little this may be clear to the majority of its disciples, most of whom have accepted this belief out of an instinct of self-preservation), but he only asserts that there is an objective connection acting from within, between various forms and manifestations of life.

The Travel Diary of a Philosopher
COUNT HERMANN KEYSERLING

RELIGION

The aim of religion is the search for God and truth. And exactly as art stops, so religion stops also as soon as it ceases to search for God and truth, thinking it has found them.

Tertium Organum
P. D. OUSPENSKY

The entire body of teachings of religio-philosophic movements have as their avowed or hidden purpose, the expansion of consciousness.

Tertium Organum
P. D. Ouspensky

As one can ascend to the top of a house by means of a ladder or a bamboo or a staircase or a rope, so diverse are the ways and means to approach God, and every religion in the world shows one of these ways.

The Works of Sri Ramakrishna
(Hindu Scriptures)
The Bible of the World

[A concept is] an image or picture by which we endeavor to make things clearer to ourselves . . . to understand them. . . . In science, when her concepts, her working hypotheses cease to keep step with observed facts, they are ruthlessly discharged. I submit we might do as well to follow the example of our scientific friends, and enquire whether a number of concepts which have so long dominated ethical and religious thought are not in need of revision.

The Human Situation
W. Macneile Dixon

Mysticism is the source itself of every creed; all the founders of great religions were mystics; and their religions are at heart attempts to bring the beatific state to every man. Mysticism explains all religions, all antique mysteries, and perhaps even such exotic sects as those of the Alchemists and the Rosicrucians.

William Blake: His Philosophy and Symbols
S. Foster Damon

All religious belief has only one significance, that of leading to self-realization; it means the imaginative exposition of being, the mirror of the centre of being in our consciousness.

The Travel Diary of a Philosopher
COUNT HERMANN KEYSERLING

However men approach me, even so do I welcome them, for the path men take from every side is mine.

The Bhagavad-Gita (Hindu Scriptures)
The Bible of the World

The test by which the mystic is positively recognized, is the ecstasy. During such moments he enters a peculiar state of mental illumination, in which he is exalted above the world as we know it, into a super sensuous state, where he is violently united with Ultimate Truth. "He may call it God, Beauty, Law, or any other name; but it is always One, and always Truth." This union with the One combines pain and pleasure, emotion and knowledge, nature and supernature, body and soul, man and God. Those who have experienced it . . . can imagine no other state of existence; and generally their whole lives thereafter are devoted to revealing on earth this ineffable secret.

William Blake: His Philosophy and Symbols
S. FOSTER DAMON

REPRESSION

It is repression only which makes the natural ugly.

America Set Free
COUNT HERMANN KEYSERLING

REQUIREMENT

To whomsoever much is given, of him shall much be required.

JESUS
Luke 12:48

RESERVE

We should show our reverence for certain mysteries by our reserve, even though it were possible to reveal them.

JOHANN WOLFGANG VON GOETHE

REVERENCE

Reverence, which no man brings into the world with him, is yet that upon which everything depends, if man is to become a man in every sense.

JOHANN WOLFGANG VON GOETHE

REVOLUTION

This is the cause which leads to the great revolutions in human history. Whenever the part, spurning the whole, tries to run a separate course of its own, the great pull of the all gives it a violent wrench, stops it suddenly, and brings it to the dust. Whenever the individual tries to dam the ever-flowing current of world-force, and imprison it within the area of his particular use, it brings on disaster. However powerful a king may be, he cannot raise his standard of rebellion against the infinite source of strength, which is unity, and yet remain powerful.

Sadhana
RABINDRANATH TAGORE

RHYTHM

Everything flows out and in; everything has its tides; all things rise and fall; pendulum swing manifests in everything; the measure of the swing to the right is the measure of the swing to the left; rhythm compensates.

The Kabalion
HERMES TRISMEGISTUS

SACRIFICE

Sacrifice is the law of the world, and nothing can be gained without it: Neither mastery here, nor possession of the heavens beyond.

RABINDRANATH TAGORE

SCIENCE

Science is only the grammar of the world, but we must master it to be able to speak.

The World in the Making
COUNT HERMANN KEYSERLING

Science is analytical description.

The Story of Philosophy
WILL DURANT

Science is like a man who knows nothing of the machinery of a motor car save the effect of moving this or that lever. It is a study of surfaces, and the probable sequence of events from the observation of previous sequences. For the rest, to be exact, it knows precisely nothing.

The Human Situation
W. MACNEILE DIXON

There was a time when we prayed for special concessions, we expected that the laws of nature should be held in abeyance for our own convenience. But now we know better. We know that law cannot be set aside, and in this knowledge we have become strong. For this law is not something apart from us; it is our own. The universal power which is manifested in the universal law is one with our own power. It will thwart us when we are small, where we are against the current of things; but it will help us where we are great, where we are in unison with the all. Thus, through the help of science, as we come to know more of the laws of nature, we gain in power; we tend to attain a universal body.

Sadhana
RABINDRANATH TAGORE

The Greeks were accustomed to speak of the peripeteia, the change or reversal of fortune or circumstances which marked the turning point in a drama. Such a peripeteia took place about the beginning of the present century, a crisis, which though many workers are hardly even now aware of the conclusion, shook the citadel of scientific thought to its foundations, and as a philosophy, left it in ruins. Science stumbled upon the vital mysteries, and awoke to the true situation. Of this revolution Relativity theory and Quantum theory were merely the heralds. It displays itself, and is in fact, the discovery by men of science of the metaphysical assumptions in all their reasoning, the least expected and by far the most momentous of their many and brilliant discoveries.

The Human Situation
W. MACNEILE DIXON

The aim of science is to foresee and not, as has often been said, to understand. Science describes facts, objects and phenomena minutely, and tries to join them by what we call laws, so as to be able to predict events in the future. For instance, by studying the motions of the heavenly bodies, astronomy has succeeded in establishing laws which enable us to calculate the position of these bodies with respect to the earth in an unlimited future.

Human Destiny
LECOMTE DU NOÜY

SECURITY

We talk about security and "safety first," when everything around us tells that "to play safe" may prove as dangerous as the most reckless gambling. There are two types of people who get run over—the timid and the reckless.

The Challenge of Change
G. A. R. WYLIE

SELF

The first thought of the human being is "I." Until you have thought "I," you cannot think "thou" or "he," or "we," or "you," or "they" . . . Gradually you will find that the thought of "I" vanishes. What is left is the Eternal Self. The self of all creation, which is beauty and bliss.

The Vedanta described by the Chidambaram Swami
Lancer at Large
FRANCIS YEATS-BROWN

How can a man come to know himself? Never by thinking, but by doing.

Life and Character
JOHANN WOLFGANG VON GOETHE

Man is indeed abroad to satisfy needs which are more to him than food and clothing. He is out to find himself.

Sadhana
RABINDRANATH TAGORE

It is a great error to take oneself for more than one is, or for less than one is worth.

Life and Character
JOHANN WOLFGANG VON GOETHE

Each should preserve the right to live according to his own soul, to walk his own way, to seek his own truth, to secure if need be his own field of activity—to carry out, in a word, the proper law of his own spiritual life, and not sacrifice himself to the law of another; even the dearest person of all; for no one has the right to violate another's soul, or his own for the sake of another. It is a crime.

ROMAIN ROLLAND

Self-reproach was a sensation wholly unknown to Goethe.

Goethe: The History of a Man
EMIL LUDWIG

To think thoughts other than one's own, to be like one's neighbor, or to meddle with his affairs? That leads to self-destruction and no one benefits by it. The first duty is to be what one is.

ROMAIN ROLLAND

Let everyone endeavor to be what he was made. . . . If a man does not keep pace with his companions, perhaps it is because he hears a different drummer. Let him step to the music which he hears, however measured and far away.

Walden
HENRY DAVID THOREAU

[To] see something wrong in self-consciousness . . . is justified when it comes to questions of political tact, physical grace, or athletic fitness. But intellectually and spiritually, there is only one line of advance—through increasing consciousness.

COUNT HERMANN KEYSERLING

A man who raises himself on tiptoe cannot remain firm.

Chinese Proverb

Self-pity is a person's most deadly enemy.

MISS MARJORIE LAWRENCE
Metropolitan Opera Singer
Adelaide Hawley Radio Program

SELF-DETERMINATION

The hour has come to take self-determination absolutely in earnest.

The Travel Diary of a Philosopher
COUNT HERMANN KEYSERLING

SELF-RELIANCE

When . . . sticks prop one another, none or only one, stands erect.

Thoreau's Journal, Oct. 1855
HENRY DAVID THOREAU

It is never right to lean on other people.

The House of Fulfilment
L. ADAMS BECK

Be ye lamps unto yourselves! Be ye a refuge to yourselves.

The last words of Lord Buddha
From Lancer at Large
FRANCIS YEATS-BROWN

Be ye lamps unto yourselves. . . . Hold fast to the truth as a lamp. Look not for refuge to anyone beside yourself.

The Bible

If a man cannot lift a stone himself, let him leave it, even though he has someone to help him.

Life and Character
JOHANN WOLFGANG VON GOETHE

Hereafter every man must want to be his own savior. This holds true—as I especially want to emphasize—even under the premise which I personally accept, that in the last analysis the decision lies with higher powers . . .

Only when a large enough number of individuals have solved their personal problems, can there ensue through this medium a molecular transposition of the whole.

The World in the Making
COUNT HERMANN KEYSERLING

SERENITY

Anchored in that serenity which, out of its strength, can accept in joy all the world's pain.

Europe
COUNT HERMANN KEYSERLING

SEX

A positivist would strive to explain . . . very simply. Singing [of birds] acts as an attraction between the females and the males, and so forth. But even a positivist will not be in a position to deny that there is a good deal more of this singing than is necessary for "the continuation of the species." For a positivist, indeed, "singing" is merely "an accident," a "by-product." But in reality it may be that this singing is the principal function of a given species, the realization of its existence, the purpose pursued by nature in creating this species; and that this singing is necessary, not so much to attract the females, as for some general harmony of nature which we only rarely and imperfectly sense.

Tertium Organum
P. D. OUSPENSKY

In the actual state of our knowledge it is impossible to attribute a precedence to such or such an organism with respect to such another, and all the more to derive one from another. All we can say is that a series of unknown phenomena ended in the appearance of very elementary algae, which still exist today, the Cyanophyceae or blue algae. In some of these, the marvelous chlorophyl is not yet present. Their pigment is a phycocyanin. These plants resemble the bacteria by their tubular or spherical form and by the sexual reproduction. They perfect themselves [?] and one day there is a great advance: The green algae invade the waters with, at last, the hope and the possibility of a conceivable evolution. They have a nucleus—which is a kind of miracle—and it seems that they inaugurate sexual reproduction—another miracle. Do the green algae with a cellular structure and a nucleus really derive from the blue algae? We cannot affirm it. At any rate the difference between the two is tremendous and the mechanisms of transition again inconceivable. But, in the negative, what could be their origin?

In any event, the progress is considerable. For even if several methods of sexual reproduction are known in plants and in animals (in a certain worm for example) it is evident that these processes reproduce indefinitely the same characters. The cell or the organism separates into two individuals who live, grow, and in their turn each separate into others (mitosis, fission, budding, etc.). They never die, except accidentally. They go on untiringly doubling their number according to their specific rhythm, so that if it were not checked by a more general or dominant phenomenon, they would soon smother the earth under their mass.

It seems logical that progress and rapid evolution can only be assured by the mixture of different strains, developed in varying environments, and by the confusion of the hereditary modifications. As sexual cells do not know death as individuals, they are immortal. All of a sudden, with sexual generation we see the appearance of an entirely new and unforeseen cyclical phenomenon, the birth and death of the individual: It is clear that sexual reproduction with fecundation, which suppresses the immortality of the individual, was indispensable to make a strain progress toward complexity. It was necessary to modify, to enrich heredity by the mixture of foreign strains, by the pooling of acquired characters.

This is an immense revolution as important and incomprehensible as the appearance of mammals. . . . This notion of the role of the individual is fundamental, and seems to introduce, from the very beginning, a distinct difference between inorganic matter and life.

Human Destiny
LECOMTE DU NOÜY

SIGNIFICANCE

Man can be happy in prison when suffering for his convictions. He may find bliss in martyrdom. But let us leave martyrs and heroes alone: even in the humblest and least heroic of lives, facts as such are never essential, once the accent is laid on significance. From that moment, the flow of life itself—however tragic it may seem to him who places all his attention on the sounds that perish and not on the melody which this series of deaths serve to create—from that moment, even infirm old age and even death no longer means a misfortune; this flow is accepted as the normal and necessary frame of human existence, and the whole accent will fall on the meaning the facts of life have.

Problems of Personal Life
COUNT HERMANN KEYSERLING

SILENCE

I keep silent about many things, for I do not want to put people out of countenance.

JOHANN WOLFGANG VON GOETHE

SIMPLICITY

Simplicity in the means employed is a sign of excellence. To simplify is to have knowledge: To complicate is to be ignorant.

The Story-book of Science
JEAN HENRI FABRE

[Sibelius] spoke of simplicity as the fundamental basis of all his aesthetic ideas.

Sibelius
BENGT DE TÖRNE

Beauty of style and harmony and grace and good rhythm depend on simplicity.

PLATO

Order and simplification are the steps toward the mastery of a subject.

The Magic Mountain
THOMAS MANN

Schopenhauer has said, that it is always a sign of genius to treat difficult matters simply, as it is a sign of dullness to make simple matters appear recondite.

Tertium Organum
P. D. Ouspensky

What you call bareness and poverty, is to me simplicity. . . . I love the winter, with its imprisonment and its cold, for it impels the prisoner to try new fields and new resources. I love to have the river close up for the season, and a pause put to my boating, to be obliged to get my boat in. I shall launch it again in the spring with so much more pleasure. This is an advantage in the point of abstinence and moderation, compared with the seaside boating, where the boat ever lies on the shore. I love best to have each thing in its season, and enjoy doing without it all the other times.

Thoreau's Journal, Dec. 5, 1856
Henry David Thoreau

SIN

Sloth is everywhere; the one and only mortal sin.

The Recovery of Truth
Count Hermann Keyserling

Inertia is the law of matter as opposed to the spirit; of all vices it is the worst.

America Set Free
Count Hermann Keyserling

SINCERITY

Sincerity is the way of heaven. The attainment of sincerity is the way of men. He who possesses sincerity is he who, without an effort, hits what is right, and apprehends without the exercise of thought; he is the sage who naturally and easily embodies the right way. He who attains to sincerity is he who chooses what is good, and firmly holds it fast. To this attainment there are requisite the extensive study of what is good, accurate inquiry about it, careful reflection on it, the clear discrimination of it, and earnest practice of it.

Chung Yung
(The Doctrine of the Steadfast Mean; Confucianist Scriptures)
The Bible of the World

SOUL

That wild swan, the soul.

The Human Situation
W. MACNEILE DIXON

What is commonly called "soul" is nothing else than the organism of the emotions.

Problems of Personal Life
COUNT HERMANN KEYSERLING

He who ruleth his own soul is greater than he who taketh a city.

Upanishads, quoted in
Indian Philosophy and Modern Culture
PAUL BRUNTON

One and the same soul is concealed within all things.

Upanishads, quoted in
Indian Philosophy and Modern Culture
PAUL BRUNTON

Leonardo supposes that not only man, but that animals, even plants, each possesses a soul.

The Romance of Leonardo da Vinci
DMITRI MEREJKOWSKI

Minerals have souls.

The Kabalion
HERMES TRISMEGISTUS

Feckner believed that human life, and I would add animal and plant life, are the sense organs of the earth soul.

The House of Fulfilment
L. ADAMS BECK

When a man has reached a certain stage of development of the soul . . . he feels the happiness of the neighboring peoples as his own.

ROMAIN ROLLAND

Patience for the insulted is the same as clothes for the chilled. In proportion as the cold increaseth, dress thyself warmer, and thou shalt not feel the cold. Just so, during great injustices increase thy patience, and the injustice shall not touch thy soul.

The Romance of Leonardo da Vinci
DMITRI MEREJKOWSKI

In the great western continent we see that the soul of man is merely concerned with extending itself outward. . . . In our country [India] . . . our partiality is for the internal world. . . . But true spirituality as taught in our secret lore, is calmly balanced in strength, in the correlation of the within and the without.

Sadhana
RABINDRANATH TAGORE

The soul of man is not yet awake, not by millenniums, and his religious and ethical codes are no more than stammering efforts to speak a language imperfectly known.

The Human Situation
W. MACNEILE DIXON

Startle the soul into admiration, ask of it the impossible, to join the forlorn hope, and it is endowed with angelic strength. Ask of it nothing, and the soul retires. Enters in its place the captious, querulous, resisting, arguing, quarrelsome intellect.

The Human Situation
W. MACNEILE DIXON

There is some hidden mystery which proceeds between God and the soul. This is experienced by those who achieve the highest heights of perfect purity of love and faith, when man changing completely unites with God.

Theognis
Tertium Organum
P. D. OUSPENSKY

Anyone who has common sense will remember that the bewilderments of the eyes are of two kinds, and arise from two causes, either from coming out of the light or from going into the light, which is true of the mind's eye, quite as much as the bodily eye; and he who remembers this when he sees the soul of anyone whose vision is perplexed and weak, will not be too ready to laugh; he will first ask whether that soul has come out of the brighter life, and is unable to see because unaccustomed to the dark, or having turned from darkness to day is dazzled by excess of light.

Plato's Republic, quoted in
Tertium Organum
P. D. OUSPENSKY

Family life is necessary to man in order that he may attain the full blossoming out of . . . the soul, understood as the organism of the higher feelings. Man literally dishumanizes when his emotional being withers. So must we oppose to the imperative of these generations which shout: No sentiment! the contrary and better imperative: Let us cultivate emotional and sentimental cohesion from man to man as no generation ever did before.

Problems of Personal Life
COUNT HERMANN KEYSERLING

SPIRIT

The word spiritual can only be correctly applied to that which belongs to the region of significance.

Creative Understanding
COUNT HERMANN KEYSERLING

The letter killeth, but the spirit giveth light.

PAUL
II Corinthians 3:6

In no case are emotions merely organs of feeling for feeling's sake; they are all organs of knowledge. In every emotion man knows something he could not know without its aid. . . . Thus "spirituality" is a fusion of the intellect with the higher emotions.

Tertium Organum
P. D. OUSPENSKY

A man who perfects himself in devotion, finds springing up in himself spiritual knowledge.

The Bhagavad-Gita (Hindu Scriptures)
The Bible of the World

Spirit which does not permeate matter is not realised as spirit. It is for the sake of the spirit that the word must be made flesh.

America Set Free
COUNT HERMANN KEYSERLING

Only the conquest of matter as it has been achieved in our days could, in principle, lead to the sovereign of the spirit on our earth. Thus present-day materialism represents in principle the very threshold of a deeper spirituality.

America Set Free
COUNT HERMANN KEYSERLING

The two most fatal errors of the Christian era were the creation and the perpetuation of these two prejudices; firstly, that all those things that do not spring from spiritual origin or cannot be reduced into terms of spirit are evils, which must be suppressed; and secondly, that all facts can be transformed through spiritual initiative.

Problems of Personal Life
COUNT HERMANN KEYSERLING

Common men accept spiritual tyrannies, weak men repine at them, and great men break them down.

GEORGE SANTAYANA

Goethe regarded all unprofitable agitations as superfluous, because to him the inexorable [unyielding] was the only school for the spirit.

Goethe: The History of a Man
EMIL LUDWIG

Let us recognize once and for all, that economic, legal, political and military necessities are to the ideal aspirations of spirit, what the kind of life proper for the bowels is for the thinking brain. From that moment illusion will disappear. But we will no longer either be exposed to disillusions leading to catastrophes. . . . From the moment we have understood once and for all which are the things refractory to all spiritualization, we will no longer ask apple trees for oranges, as Flaubert used to say. The law of the belly, as long as its aspirations are maintained within their normal limits, has never prevented any man from philosophising. . . . We can so ground our vital center in spirit, which is superior to nature, that natural needs will play no greater part than that of rain or fine weather.

Problems of Personal Life
COUNT HERMANN KEYSERLING

The most profound error and the worst sin in the Christian sense has ever been the inner consent to illusion. . . . We ought to cease believing in sacred rights, and particularly in the sacred rights of property; we ought to cease believing in the possible morality of good politics, and in the possibility of idealistic business.

We must admit once and for all that the lower depths of man are an expression of Evil when viewed from the vantage ground of spirit.

Problems of Personal Life
COUNT HERMANN KEYSERLING

The spirit is smothered, as it were, by ignorance, but so soon as ignorance is destroyed, spirits shines forth, like the sun when released from clouds. After the soul, afflicted by ignorance, has been purified by knowledge, knowledge disappears, as the seed or berry of the Kataka after it has purified water.

ATMA BODHA OF SANKARACHARYA
(*Knowledge of Spirit in Hinduism*)
The Bible of the World

The plane proper to spirit is imagination.

COUNT HERMANN KEYSERLING

Let intellectuals doubt spiritual reality as much as they please; there has never, in fact, been any man who has universally been recognized as Superior who has not tried to realize in himself Goodness, Beauty, Love and Sincerity and who has not felt unhappy if he did not feel his activity to be at the service of spiritual ideals. In a like way each normally endowed human being feels as a matter of course that material success or failure neither prove nor disprove the validity of eternal values. It is because they belong to an entirely different dimension. Summarizing the essential in one brief formula; Man does what is right in order to become better; he aspires toward beauty in order to attain perfect self-expression; to Truth, in order to free his own inner reality from all that is unreal.

Problems of Personal Life
COUNT HERMANN KEYSERLING

Spirit is dynamic, and must be able to grow and change, according to inner necessity.

"Will We Continue to Have Monogamous Marriage?" (*A lecture*)
COUNT HERMANN KEYSERLING

Society as a whole can be changed not by social laws and by social obligations, but by inner spiritual development.

Lecture, 1928
COUNT HERMANN KEYSERLING

The spirit principle, being opposed to the law of matter, will not endure executive routine.

America Set Free
COUNT HERMANN KEYSERLING

Never the spirit was born; the spirit shall cease to be never.

Never was time it was not. End and beginning are dreams.

Deathless and birthless and changeless abideth the spirit forever.

Death cannot touch it at all, dead though the house of it seems.

Katha Upanishad (Hindu Scriptures)
The Bible of the World

SPIRITUALISM

My sister, H. P. Blavatsky, had passed most of her time, during her many years' absence from Russia, traveling in India, where as we are informed, spiritual theories are held in great scorn, and the so-called (by us) mediumistic phenomena are said to be caused by quite another agency than that of spirits; mediumship proceeds they say, from a source to draw from which, my sister thinks, is degrading to her human dignity.

Personal and Family Reminiscences
(Incidents in the life of Mme. Blavatsky)
MME. JELIHOWSKY

STILLNESS

Be still and know that I am God.

Psalm 46:10

Keep still and help will come to you.

Proverb

Nothing is made fruitful save by time and silence.

ROMAIN ROLLAND

A pool ruffled by the wind cannot reflect the stars.

The Chidambaram Swami
Lancer at Large
FRANCIS YEATS-BROWN

Muddy water . . . if permitted to remain still . . . will gradually become clear of itself.

Chinese Proverb

SUCCESS

There can be no question of material success or failure proving or disproving the validity of the eternal values or ideas; they belong to an altogether different dimension.

America Set Free
COUNT HERMANN KEYSERLING

Start where you are, with what you have, make something of it, never be satisfied.

GEORGE WASHINGTON CARVER
Reader's Digest, 1942

Now understand me well. It is provided in the essence of things that from any fruition of success, no matter what, shall come forth something to make a greater struggle necessary.

WALT WHITMAN

Whenever a man is universally and unanimously acclaimed, it only means that those who acclaim him do not really consider him superior to themselves—which explains why they can bring themselves to deify him.

Europe
COUNT HERMANN KEYSERLING

We must walk consciously only part way towards our goal, and then leap in the dark to our success.

Thoreau's Journal, March 11, 1859
HENRY DAVID THOREAU

A quotation, a chance word heard in an unexpected quarter, puts me on the trail of the book destined to achieve an intellectual advancement in me.

GEORGE MOORE

It is only men of practical ability, knowing their powers and using them with moderation and prudence, who will be successful in worldly affairs.

Life and Character
JOHANN WOLFGANG VON GOETHE

SUPERIORITY

That which makes superiority is the ability to see things in their right proportion and to rule them from within so as to produce a harmonious general state.

America Set Free
COUNT HERMANN KEYSERLING

The master by rising mentally to the higher plane [escapes] the swing of the mental pendulum . . . manifest in the lower plane. . . .

Nothing escapes the principle of cause and effect, but there are many planes of causation, and one may use the laws of the higher to overcome the laws of the lower.

The Kabalion
HERMES TRISMEGISTUS

TEMPTATION

When temptation comes, it often comes, as it were, of a sudden, before the mind has time to become aware of what is happening. One is apparently hurried on to the point of yielding. All saints understood this. Therefore they anticipate evil thought, defeating its strength and the possibility of its arising by strenuous good thought.

In the Hour of Meditation
F. J. ALEXANDER

THANKFULNESS

One word of thanks reaches up to heaven.

Japanese Proverb

THINE

I came to offer Thee a flower,
But Thou must have all my garden.
It is Thine.

RABINDRANATH TAGORE

Thou hast made us for thyself,
And our heart is restless until it rests in Thee.

SAINT AUGUSTINE

THINGS

I saw that everything was Divine.

In the Hour of Meditation
F. J. ALEXANDER

Our misfortune consists in the fact that we regard the chemical constitution of a thing as its most real attribute, while as a matter of fact its true attributes must be sought for in its functions.

Tertium Organum
P. D. Ouspensky

Things are united, not by time, but by an inner connection, an inner correlation. And time cannot separate those things which are inwardly near, following one from another.

Tertium Organum
P. D. Ouspensky

A thing may acquire its own individual and unique soul; and in that case the thing exists quite independently of our receptivity. Many things possess such souls, especially old things, old houses, old books, works of art, etc.

Tertium Organum
P. D. Ouspensky

We know that everything exists in infinite spaces of time, nothing is made, nothing becomes, all is. But we do not see everything at once, and therefore it seems to us that everything moves, grows, is becoming. We do not see everything at once, either in the outer world, or in the inner world; thence arises the illusion of motion.

Tertium Organum
P. D. Ouspensky

THOUGHT

No man can do more for others than stimulate them to independent, original thought.

The Recovery of Truth
Count Hermann Keyserling

He saw that no sincere thought could be wholly untrue, and therefore could not be wholly rejected.

William Blake: His Philosophy and Symbols
S. Foster Damon

Every man must think after his own fashion; for on his own path he finds a truth, or a kind of truth, which helps him through life.

Life and Character
Johann Wolfgang von Goethe

The mystery of thought creates all. As soon as we shall understand that thought is not a "function of motion," but that motion itself is only a function of thought—and shall begin to feel the depth of this mystery—we shall perceive that the entire phenomenal world is some gigantic hallucination, which fails to frighten us.

Tertium Organum
P. D. Ouspensky

True motion that lies at the foundation of everything, is the motion of thought. True energy is the energy of consciousness; and truth itself is motion, and can never lead to arrestment, to the cessation of search.

Tertium Organum
P. D. Ouspensky

Man made of thought . . . is eternally thinking. His chains are through thought, his release due to nothing else.

Notes on Bhagavad-Gita
William Judge *and* Robert Crosbie

The fact is that thought and energy are different in substance and cannot be one and the same thing, because they are different sides of one and the same thing.

Tertium Organum
P. D. Ouspensky

Thought is useless for thinking: Those thoughts which give true expression to an inner and outer reality on their own plane "occur"; they are every time the fruit, or the product of an intimate vital experience.

Johann Wolfgang von Goethe

I think the day is near at hand on which men will think it one of the most absurd errors of human history to have claimed that a thinker as such can solve ontological problems or those of existence. The problems and legitimate radius of action of the "thinker" comprises but the formal side of thought, that is to say, logic and mathematical abstraction. There is still epistemology, but this, handled by "pure" thinkers, easily goes astray, for, after all, true understanding concerns concrete experiences and not the formal conditions which lead to them; and the "thinker" type is essentially lacking in all sense of reality.

Problems of Personal Life
Count Hermann Keyserling

When we come upon infinity in any mode of our thought, it is a sign that that mode of thought is dealing with a higher reality than it is adapted for.

Tertium Organum
P. D. Ouspensky

My thought is a part of the meaning of the world, and I use a part of the world as a symbol to express my thought.

Thoreau's Journal, Nov. 4, 1852
Henry David Thoreau

Learning without thought is labor lost: Thought without learning is perilous.

CONFUCIUS

Thought needs a fulcrum for its lever, effort demands an incentive or an aim.

The Human Situation
W. MACNEILE DIXON

"Looking beyond the moment," is the essence of the epic, the broad symphonic outlook: it means thinking in perspective.

Sibelius
BENGT DE TÖRNE

Thought greets thought over the widest gulfs of time, with unerring freemasonry. I know for instance, that Sadi entertained once identically the same thought as I do. He is not Persian, he is not ancient, he is not strange to me. By the identity of his thoughts with mine, he still survives. It makes no odds what atoms serve us. Sadi possesses no greater privacy or individuality than is thrown open to me. He had no more interior and essential and sacred self than came naked into my thoughts this moment.

Thoreau's Journal
HENRY DAVID THOREAU

The relationship between Western and Eastern thought is the same as empiric and metaphysical life, [but] they must consciously be interrelated in that way. Our Occidental spiritual body properly adjusted and perfectly developed would be the very body required for the best possible expression of that very spiritual reality which in itself and as such has been recognized by the East.

Creative Understanding
COUNT HERMANN KEYSERLING

TIME

The present is not a sizeable moment, it is continuously transitory into the past. . . .

The past and future cannot not exist, because if they do not exist, then neither does the present exist. Unquestionably they exist somewhere together but we do not see them.

Tertium Organum
P. D. OUSPENSKY

Time is the fourth dimension of space.

Tertium Organum
P. D. OUSPENSKY

The reality of time also consists in imagination. As there is no real Extension in space so there is no duration of time apart from the activity of the mind. One night of a tormented creature passes as an age, whereas it is experienced as a moment in the merriment of the happy. If within a moment one could imagine the whole cycle of the world's existence, the moment would actually be experienced as a moment through imagination.

Vivishta, quoted in
Indian Philosophy and Modern Culture
PAUL BRUNTON

For everything beneath the sun there is a season and a time.

Lavengro
GEORGE BORROW

Time is motionless and people travel through it.

Tertium Organum
P. D. OUSPENSKY

Fireworks at noon have no effect at all.

JOHANN WOLFGANG VON GOETHE

Everything must wait its turn—peach blossoms for the second month, and chrysanthemums for the ninth.

Japanese Proverb

TOLERANCE

He that is without sin among you, let him first cast a stone at her.

JESUS
John 8:7

Live and let live.

English Gypsy

Tolerance is a symbol of strength.

ALBERT SPALDING
Radio, Aug. 17, 1943

As [the Chinese] philosophers have said, "To be lenient to oneself but severe to the faults of others, intolerance. To be lenient to the faults of others, for in a mirror is always a reflection—tolerance."

Three Times I Bow
CARL GLICK

The lotus grows out of the mud without being spoiled thereby. If I am not mistaken there was one of our own great teachers who was not afraid to consort with fallen women and thieves.

Three Times I Bow
CARL GLICK

TRUST

Trust creates trust, and the state which is worthy of it.

Ancient Chinese Wisdom

All power is trust, and we are accountable for its exercise.

BENJAMIN DISRAELI,
EARL OF BEACONSFIELD

TRUTH

Man is incapable of grasping pure truth in its entirety. The very search for it, uncompromising, and conducted in humility, constitutes the most intimate contact with eternal variety which he will ever know. Exposed to this search in the mind and heart of another, he is exalted and feels the cleansing breath of truth itself, even though the other's point of view may differ radically in details from his own. And he will find, too, strangely insistent notes of that cosmic music of the soul the elusiveness of which has always tortured his desire.

Introduction to
The Bible of the World
ROBERT O. BALLOU

It is much easier to recognize error than to find truth; for error lies on the surface and may be overcome; but truth lies in the depths, and to search for it is not given to everyone.

Life and Character
JOHANN WOLFGANG VON GOETHE

Truth is at variance with our natures, but not so error, and for a very simple reason. Truth requires us to recognize ourselves as limited, but error flatters us with the belief that in one way or another we are subject to no bonds at all.

Life and Character
JOHANN WOLFGANG VON GOETHE

When I was young I was happy, I thought truth was something that could be conveyed from one man's mind to another. I now know it is a state of mind.

THE BRAHAM MOHINI

A soul which has seen truth, and seeks to deny truth, destroys itself.

ROMAIN ROLLAND

Don't tell the truth if it hurts another.

Lecture
COUNT HERMANN KEYSERLING

Seek out your own truth and realize it. There is no ready-made truth, no rigid formula, which one person can hand over to another. Each must create truth for himself and according to his own model.

ROMAIN ROLLAND

Ignorant men who had no access to books have by their inward sense perceived the real truth of things. . . .

Notes on the Bhagavad-Gita
WILLIAM JUDGE *and* ROBERT CROSBIE

Everyone must discover the truth for himself. "Another's truth" is worse than a lie, because it is two lies.

Tertium Organum
P. D. OUSPENSKY

Let us think imperially, for the more magnificent our thoughts, the nearer . . . truth.

The Human Situation
W. MACNEILE DIXON

What time and labor would be saved, and from what enormous and unnecessary suffering would humanity save itself, could it but understand this one simple thing: that truth cannot be expressed in our language. Then would men cease to think that they possessed truth, and would cease to force others to accept their truth at any cost, would see that others may approach truth from another direction, exactly as they themselves approach it, by a way of their own. How many arguments, how many religious struggles, how much of violence towards the thoughts of others would be rendered unnecessary and impossible if men would only understand that nobody possesses truth, but all are seeking for it, each in his own way!

Tertium Organum
P. D. Ouspensky

Let him comfort and persuade himself before trying to persuade others. Let him by all the means at his disposal, concentrate his will on the construction of an unshakable faith even though it be only a faith in the dignity and destiny of man. The method he employs is of no importance. We have said it before; no matter what road is chosen the travelers who started from different valleys will all meet on the top of the mountain, provided they keep on ascending. No one must pride himself on having chosen the best route nor force his neighbors to follow him. Everyone takes the path which suits him best, imposed by the structure of the brain, by heredity, by traditions. One can offer support, enlightenment, help. But what succeeds with one may fail with others, and every man must wage his own fight without which he cannot progress. There is no short cut to truth.

Sincere effort alone counts. It is that which affirms the spiritual kinship of men, and the link which it establishes between them is more real than any other. A day will come when, as a result of evolution, moral perfection latent in a small minority will blossom in the majority, as will the universal comprehension and love radiated by Christ. In the meantime, the only way to prepare for its advent is to improve man himself. By laboring to perfect himself, by building an inner temple, by judging himself without complacency, man unconsciously shapes a soul which overflows and extends all around him, anxious to diffuse in that of others. By seeking himself he finds his brother.

Human Destiny
LECOMTE DU NOÜY

It is a far greater achievement to face a hard truth than to be optimistic in spite of everything.

America Set Free
COUNT HERMANN KEYSERLING

UNDERSTANDING

Understanding has nothing to do with explanation. It is not subject to the law of cause and effect. It is a direct union between spirit and spirit, or soul and soul, or flesh and flesh.

America Set Free
COUNT HERMANN KEYSERLING

The lower can never comprehend the higher . . . while the higher may comprehend the lower.

Intuition
WALTER NEWELL WESTON

[Only] Buddha in the whole course of history, understood the full importance of the fact that thought, or more precisely understanding, is the thing most needful on earth. He used his understanding for the purpose of destroying the world. But it can be used for the purpose of raising the world to a higher level.

The Recovery of Truth
COUNT HERMANN KEYSERLING

It is impossible to know through impure emotions. Therefore in the interests of a correct understanding of the world and of the self, man should undertake the purification and the elevation of his emotions.

Tertium Organum
P. D. Ouspensky

Speaking generally, information is desirable only after you know, never before; understanding alone means true knowledge; and understanding can never be derived from information.

America Set Free
Count Hermann Keyserling

Understanding is the greatest force man commands.

America Set Free
Count Hermann Keyserling

One may know everything and yet understand nothing or else understand everything without knowing anything.

Problems of Personal Life
Count Hermann Keyserling

I can see only one way leading to salvation; with the greatest force imaginable, we must accentuate personal understanding in opposition to knowledge which can become general.

Problems of Personal Life
Count Hermann Keyserling

UNIQUENESS

Consider that this day ne'er dawns again.

Dante Alighieri

The hole the crab digs takes on the shape of the shell.

Japanese Proverb

Let us . . . then, have the courage to be and to declare ourselves unique! Let us have the courage to place all our available energies at the service of our uniqueness. Then every life, even the humblest, even the least happy one, from the external point of view, will have a profound and intrinsic significance. Let us cultivate the courage and the faith needed to live a profoundly personal existence.

Problems of Personal Life
COUNT HERMANN KEYSERLING

UNITY

All that exists is one, though sages call it by different names.

Vedas

There is no within, there is no without, for what is within is also without.

JOHANN WOLFGANG VON GOETHE

The fire which enlightens is also the fire which consumes.

Journal
HENRI FRÉDÉRIC AMIEL

With Sir Jagadis (Bose) it is not a theory that all life is one: it is a scientific fact: there is a provable basis of unity, in composition, structure, reaction to outer stimulus, that runs through all matter. A plant needs sleep, glories in sunlight, winces when struck. Even a steel girder will grow tired of its burden. These things he has drawn out in diagrams and charted in graphs by means of instruments of marvellous delicacy and precision.

Lancer at Large
FRANCIS YEATS-BROWN

Twentieth century laboratories have begun to confirm the tremendous idea that there is one universal substance which forms the basis of our entire material universe. Radioactive phenomena constituted the first key to this discovery. A further key was fashioned when the nuclei of hydrogen and helium were shot into the nuclei of other atoms, and the dream of transmuting basic elements was at last realized. More recently, matter as represented by electrons, has been converted into light, as has been represented by photon and vice-versa.

The work of the physicists like Curie, Rutherford, Fermi, Cockcroft, Chadwick, Anderson and Millikan has brought us to the practical and proven scientific principal that the inner structure of matter is energy which is the "life" of the myriad forms that make up our universe. It now seems likely modern developments in the laboratory will vindicate the theory of a single element underlying all nature . . . assertions of ancient Hindu philosophers.

Indian Philosophy and Modern Culture
PAUL BRUNTON

Into the pervading genius we pass . . . and thenceforth each is all in God. There is no higher, no deeper, no other than the life in which we are founded. The one remains, the many change and pass; and each and every one of us, is the one that remains. . . . This is the ultimatum.

The Anaesthetic Revelation and the Gist of Philosophy by B. P. Blood, quoted in Tertium Organum
P. D. OUSPENSKY

The unity of the organism, the co-ordination of its parts, there you have the supreme enigma.

The Human Situation
W. MACNEILE DIXON

This search for system is really a search for unity, for synthesis; it is our attempt to harmonize the heterogeneous complexity of our outward materials by our inner adjustment. . . . The apple falls from the tree, the rain descends upon the earth—you can go on burdening your memory with such facts and never come to an end. But once you get hold of the law of gravitation you can dispense with the necessity of collecting facts ad infinitum. . . . And that is the object which the Upanishads has in view when it says, "Know thine own soul." Or, in other words, realize the one great principle of unity that there is in every man.

Sadhana
Rabindranath Tagore

UNIVERSE

The universe is mental, held in The Mind of The All. The Universe, and all it contains is a mental creation of The All.

The Kabalion
Hermes Trismegistus

The concept of the universe as a world of pure thought throws a new light on many of the situations we have encountered in our survey of modern physics.

Sir James Jeans, quoted in
Indian Philosophy and Modern Culture
Paul Brunton

There is nothing static in the universe.

The Human Situation
W. Macneile Dixon

A year or two ago Professor Einstein calculated the size of the universe. It was finite and its diameter was 216 million light-years. It now appears that his calculations may have gone astray. It may after all be infinite. One is not greatly surprised: Any one of us can tell, even you and I, that it is one or the other; yet if infinite it is not curved, for infinity has neither shape nor boundary.

The Human Situation
W. MACNEILE DIXON

We must rid ourselves of the notion that the universe is something outside ourselves to which we accidentally belong. We are the universe, in every fibre of our body and being, nerve and thought, as are all other souls, each a microcosm of that macrocosm.

The Human Situation
W. MACNEILE DIXON

The Hoyle–Lyttleton universe has no beginning, no end, and no circumference in either time or space. . . .

Hoyle, assuming that all space is filled with very thin hydrogen, has calculated that galaxies are forming continuously, and that there is "continuous creation" of hydrogen in space.

Where the hydrogen comes from—or if it comes from "anywhere" in the ordinary sense—Hoyle and his colleagues do not know. . . . When the galaxies reach the speed of light, they "just disappear." But the mass of those that go "over the edge" of perception equals exactly the mass of newly created hydrogen.

"The Universe According to Hoyle"
Time, November 20, 1950
(Reprinted in Reader's Digest, March, 1951)

USE

Wouldst thou possess thy heritage, essay
By use to render it thine own!
What we employ not but impedes the way.
That which the hour creates, that can it use alone.

Faust
Johann Wolfgang von Goethe

To look at food and say that it is good will not satisfy a starving man; he must put forth his hand and eat.

At the Feet of the Master
Jiddu Krishnamurti

VIBRATION

Principle of Vibration: Nothing rests; everything moves; everything vibrates.

He who understands the principle of vibration has grasped the sceptre of power, says one writer.

First a revolving top moves slowly and may be seen readily. It moves faster and faster, and a deep growl is heard. The note is increased, and rises into musical scale. As speed increases, it goes through the scales and then silence follows, as a rate of motion is too high for human ears to register vibrations.

Then come degrees of heat. Next colors. Then invisible rays from which electricity and magnetism are eliminated in turn.

At a certain rate of vibration molecules disintegrate and resolve themselves into original elements or atoms. Atoms are separated into countless corpuscles. Corpuscles disappear, and the object may be said to be composed of the Ethereal Substance. Science goes no further but Hermetists teach the object would manifest various mental stages until it would finally re-enter the All which is Absolute Spirit.

The Kabalion
Hermes Trismegistus

VISION

The astonishing thing about the human being is not so much his intellect and bodily structure, profoundly mysterious as they are. The astonishing thing . . . is his range of vision; his gaze into the infinite distance; his lonely passion for ideas and ideals, far removed from his material surroundings and animal activities, and in no way suggested by them, yet for which . . . he is willing to endure toils and privations, to sacrifice pleasures . . . rating them in value above his own life.

The Human Situation
W. MACNEILE DIXON

Men see things from their own angles in time and space, in conformity with their circumstances and their own individualities. How else could they see them?

The Human Situation
W. MACNEILE DIXON

A dwarf standing on the shoulders of a giant can see farther than the giant can.

The Anatomy of Melancholy
ROBERT BURTON

Again as so many times I [am] reminded of the advantage to the poet, the philosopher and the naturalist . . . of pursuing from time to time some other business than his chosen one, seeing with the side of the eye: The poet will so get visions which no deliberate abandonment can secure. The philosopher is so forced to recognize principles which long study might not detect, and the naturalist even, will stumble upon some new and unexpected flower and animal.

Thoreau's Journal, Apr. 28, 1856
HENRY DAVID THOREAU

Whoever pierces all things with a clear eye, may well do without information.

LAO-TSU

William Blake was never known to show the slightest belief in the objective reality of any vision. "Where did you see all that, Mr. Blake?" "In here." (Pointing to his forehead.)

William Blake: His Philosophy and Symbols
S. FOSTER DAMON

WEAKNESS

One profits the weak more by being strong than by sharing their weakness.

ROMAIN ROLLAND

WEALTH

Man discovers his own wealth when God comes to ask gifts of him.

RABINDRANATH TAGORE

He was one of those who didn't want millions, but an answer to their questions.

The Brothers Karamazov
FYODOR DOSTOEVSKY

The reason Jesus said "It is easier for a camel to go through the eye of a needle than for a rich man to enter the kingdom of heaven," was that wealth is apt to bring inertia.

COUNT HERMANN KEYSERLING

Every normal man or woman desires to be comfortable. Naturally so, because the highest possible standard of living is the normal ideal of the human animal. Only those very rare individuals in whom spirit predominates, and who moreover belong to the ascetic type, are genuine exceptions.

America Set Free
COUNT HERMANN KEYSERLING

Capitalism hurts you only when you use it wrongly, and turn it against your neighbor. There is no intrinsic vice in wealth: The devil is in our greed.

Barindra Ghose, quoted in
Lancer at Large
FRANCIS YEATS-BROWN

WILL

Will is the resultant of desires. We call that man strong willed in whom the will proceeds on definite lines, without turning aside; and we call that man weak-willed in whom the line of the will takes a zig-zag course, turning aside here or there under the influence of every new desire. But this does not mean that will and desire are something opposite; quite the reverse, they are one and the same, because the will is composed of desires.

Tertium Organum
P. D. OUSPENSKY

WINE

Let no one accuse me of being a Prohibitionist; God gave us the grape, and Christ Himself said that He would drink of it with His disciples in Paradise. I believe in wine as I believe in Christian chivalry, to redeem the world from drabness. But I also—and it is not illogical—believe in abstinence from wine on certain occasions.

Lancer at Large
FRANCIS YEATS-BROWN

The drunkard knows not the shame of wine—nor the abstinent its glow.

Japanese Proverb

Alcohol in all its forms has a direct, marked, and very deleterious influence on man's psychic condition. Wine and spirit drinking is only less destructive to the development of the inner powers than the habitual use of hashish, opium, and similar drugs.

The Key to Theosophy
H. P. BLAVATSKY

WISDOM

The lips of wisdom are closed, except to the ears of understanding.

The Kabalion
HERMES TRISMEGISTUS

Wise is he who knows how to learn from everyone.

The Talmud

On some of the important topics, the wisest men of the ancient East, and the modern West, starting from totally different premises, are beginning to arrive at precisely the same conclusions.

Indian Philosophy and Modern Culture
PAUL BRUNTON

To have a regard for what is possible, is . . . the beginning of wisdom. If such be the case, then clearly a perfect and everlasting happiness in the world, even if desirable, is clean out of the question. Worship perfection by all means, but do not ask for it or expect it.

The Human Situation
W. MACNEILE DIXON

He alone is wise who can see things without their individuality.

Buddhist Scriptures

We know better than we do, and we are wiser than we know.

RALPH WALDO EMERSON

The wise ones serve on the higher plane, but rule on the lower. They obey the laws coming from above them, but on their own plane, and those below them they rule and give orders. And yet in so doing, they form a part of the principle instead of opposing it. The wise man falls in with the Law, and by understanding its movements, he operates it instead of being its blind slave. Just so does the skilled swimmer turn this way and that way, going and coming as he will, instead of being as a log which is being carried here and there. So is the wise man compared to the ordinary man. And yet both swimmer and log, wise man and fool, are subject to the law. He who understands this is well on the road to mastery.

The Kabalion
HERMES TRISMEGISTUS

WORK

Mechanical work plays the part of an indispensable automatic function, like that of the heart.

Problems of Personal Life
COUNT HERMANN KEYSERLING

WORLD

The world came into existence about 2000 million years ago.

Human Destiny
LECOMTE DU NOÜY

The secret of the world's everlasting interest lies precisely here— that you cannot explain it, and never know what is going to happen next. This is the source of our unabating hope and never dying expectation.

The Human Situation
W. MACNEILE DIXON

A breath perturbed the heavens' translucence.

Buddhist idea of the beginning of the creation of worlds

Put the milk in [a cream separator], spin the bowl, and centrifugal force parts the cream quickly. There is skim milk left, plus a little froth. Now eminent geologists tell us that much the same thing happened to our earth millions of years ago. Valuable metals, the cream, all stayed inside our globe, miles below the surface. Our greatest mines like Sudbury and Trail and Flin Flan, are only specks of froth.

"Tsk, Tsk—Sudbury Is Only Froth"
H. DYOON CARTER
Saturday Night, March 15, 1941

God, then, as the mystics say, negates Himself in order that there may be a world, and this negation or sundering is creation's dawn. . . . As Bohme expresses it, "All things subsist in Yes and No."

The Human Situation
W. MACNEILE DIXON

It is very important to observe that the Vedantist does not go so far as certain Buddhist philosophers who look upon the phenomenal world as simply nothing. No, their world is real, only it is not what it seems to be.

Tertium Organum
P. D. OUSPENSKY

We have reason to think that the world is what it is of necessity, if a world there was to be.

Tertium Organum
P. D. Ouspensky

To confer significance means to superpose a new and better world upon the pre-existing one, [not] interpreting that which is already there.

Problems of Personal Life
Count Hermann Keyserling

A static world it is not, never was, and never will be. There have been revolutions in the past and there will be revolutions hereafter, in the world of thought as in the world of events.

The Human Situation
W. Macneile Dixon

We may learn to know the world as we please: There will always remain a bright and a dark side.

Life and Character
Johann Wolfgang von Goethe

Half a billion years or more ago, in the remote geological time called Pre-Cambrian, earth conditions were not essentially different from what they are now.

The Advance of Science
Formerly edited by Watson Davis
Director of Science Service

There are good, kind souls who suppose it possible to have good without evil. But liking involves disliking, and approval disapproval. The antithesis is everlasting and unavoidable. From the clash of opposites has arisen the world with all its varieties, its infinite diversity of creatures.

The Human Situation
W. Macneile Dixon

One is reminded of the profoundly significant Hellenic myth of the giant Antaeus, whose strength was perpetually renewed so long as his feet remained planted upon Mother Earth, but who became as weak as a kitten when Hercules lifted him into the air.

André Gide

WRITING

Composition . . . allows of no tricks. The best you can write will be the best you are.

Thoreau's Journal, Feb. 28, 1841
Henry David Thoreau

Be sound and thorough in all you do; think just what you think, and feel just what you feel. Let the rhythm of your heart prevail in your writings. The style is the soul.

Romain Rolland

The great epic writers like Goethe . . . never lose sight of the whole. . . . This is made possible by thinking in perspective. Lyric poets face life the opposite way. The spell of romance, the exaltation of success and the dejection of adversity completely absorb them, to the exclusion of any mental measuring capacity. Episodes in the foreground of the mind assume such color as to falsify the tones of the background.

Sibelius
Bengt de Törne

I am surprised that my affirmations or utterances came to me ready-made, not from forethought, so that I occasionally awake in the night simply to let fall a ripe statement which I had never consciously considered before.

Thoreau's Journal
Henry David Thoreau

I see that my neighbors look with compassion on me, that they think it is a mean and unfortunate destiny which makes me to walk in these fields and woods so much, and sail on the river alone. But so long as I find here the only real Elysium, I cannot hesitate in my choice. My work is writing . . . and I know that no subject is too trivial for me, tried by ordinary standards; for, ye fools, the theme is nothing, the life is everything . . . the depth and intensity of the life excited. We touch our subject but by a point which has no breadth but the pyramid of our experience, or our interest in it.

Thoreau's Journal, Oct. 18, 1856
HENRY DAVID THOREAU

The most ancient manner of writing was that by representing things by persons and by words, by which was understood something altogether different from what was expressed. In such manner, indeed, that nothing was literally true just as it was written, but under these narratives, something allegorical was understood. . . . This method of writing they, the writers of the Bible, derived from the most ancient people who lived before the flood, and who represented to themselves things heavenly and divine, by such as are visible on the earth and in the world, and thus filled their minds and souls with joyous and delightful perceptions. The most ancient people, as they had communications with spirits and angels, had no other speech than this . . . in every expression of which there is a spiritual sense.

EMANUEL SWEDENBORG

YOUTH

Parents who really love their children should want them to be independent, should do everything to encourage their originality, develop their individuality.

The Tyranny of Affection
ANDRÉ MAUROIS

The tyranny of affection is more dangerous than the tyranny of unkindness. The former makes victims of its objects; the latter makes rebels.

The Tyranny of Affection
ANDRÉ MAUROIS

Children should be brought up feeling they are loved, but will be disciplined, and young delinquents can be helped in the same way.

Author Unknown

One factor has remained the same [from your childhood], your personality. Whether you are now a "lone wolf" or a gregarious soul who works and plays best with others. . . .

As far as the laboratory has been able to determine, the extremely objective person is the born salesman. Those who average "objective" are the executives, and may turn into presidents and vice-presidents of successful companies, managers, superintendents, and department heads. The subjective youngster would do his best as a professional worker.

[One child] might test extremely subjective in personality.

It means simply . . . she is an individualist and will do her best working by herself. If her predominating aptitudes are developed, someday she may make a very definite contribution to the world.

To be well adjusted, psychologists tell us we must act the part in life nature intended us to play. If we don't, we get into trouble.

"Is Your Child Subjective?"
MARGARET BROADLY
New York Herald Tribune, Nov. 9, 1941

For the individual the way he was brought up makes a psychological difference ineradicable and not to be repaired by any kind of later self-education.

America Set Free
COUNT HERMANN KEYSERLING

The Chinese train their children with affirmatives.

Author Unknown

There is the greatest practical benefit in making a few failures in early life.

THOMAS HENRY HUXLEY

It is not well for young ideas, hardly out of the pod, to be exposed to the raw sunlight. The soul is scorched by it.

ROMAIN ROLLAND

You are young, my son, and as the years go by, time will change and even reverse many of your present opinions. Refrain therefore awhile from setting yourself up as a judge of the higher matters.

PLATO

The mentality of young artists is as a rule very complicated.

Sibelius
BENGT DE TÖRNE

The impressions of childhood form our most precious inheritance in life.

Sibelius
BENGT DE TÖRNE

A mother should give her children the background for self-development.

KASHA
Bessie Beatty Radio Broadcast,
April 2, 1941

As a wet-nurse in a rich family brings up the child of her master, loving the baby as if it were her own, but knows well that she has no claim upon it; so think ye also that ye are trustees and guardians of your children whose real father is the Lord God in heaven.

THE WORKS OF SRI RAMAKRISHNA
(Hindu Scriptures)
The Bible of the World

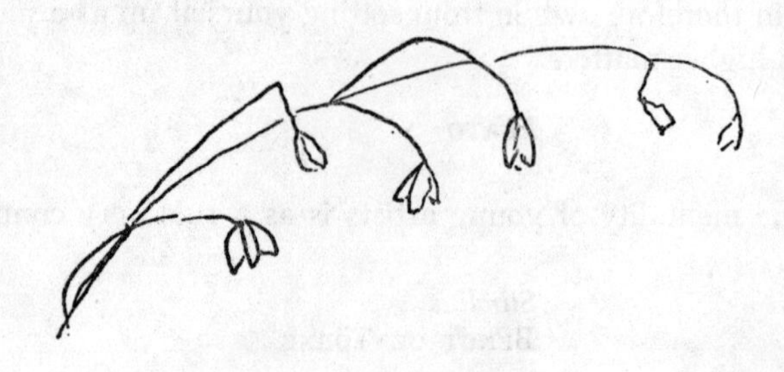

SUBJECTS

INDEX